HOW SWEET IT IS

HOW SWEET IT IS

*Defending
the American Dream*

WINSOME
EARLE-SEARS

**CENTER
STREET**

NASHVILLE • NEW YORK

Center Street
Hachette Book Group
1290 Avenue of the Americas, New York, NY 10104
centerstreet.com
twitter.com/CenterStreet

First Edition: August 2023

Center Street is a division of Hachette Book Group, Inc. The Center Street name and logo are trademarks of Hachette Book Group, Inc.

The publisher is not responsible for websites (or their content) that are not owned by the publisher.

Center Street books may be purchased in bulk for business, educational, or promotional use. For information, please contact your local bookseller or the Hachette Book Group Special Markets Department at special.markets@hbgusa.com.

All photos courtesy of the author.

Library of Congress Cataloging-in-Publication Data
Names: Earle-Sears, Winsome, author.
Title: How sweet it is : defending the American dream / Winsome Earle-Sears.
Description: First edition. | Nashville : Center Street, 2023. | Includes bibliographical references.
Identifiers: LCCN 2023008717 | ISBN 9781546004479 (hardcover) | ISBN 9781546004646 (ebook)
Subjects: LCSH: Earle-Sears, Winsome. | Lieutenant governors—Virginia—Biography. | African American women politicians—Virginia—Biography. | Jamaican American women—Virginia—Biography.
Classification: LCC F231.3.S43 A3 2023 | DDC 975.50092 [B]—dc23/eng/20230322
LC record available at https://lccn.loc.gov/2023008717

ISBN: 9781546004479 (hardcover), 9781546004646 (ebook)

Printed in the United States of America

LSC

Printing 1, 2023

DEDICATED TO:
My great-grandmother, Alberta
My grandmothers: Valda and Sylvia
My father and mother: William and Olive

My husband, Terence O. Sears
My daughters: DeJon, Katia, and Janel

But most of all
To the
God of
Abraham, Isaac, and Jacob

Do not assume that you are safe if you remain silent.

(see Esther 4:14)

CONTENTS

HOW
SWEET
IT IS

PROLOGUE

"Winsome! Winsome! Winsome! Winsome!" the crowd chanted.

We were in a hotel ballroom in Chantilly, Virginia, part of the vast Northern Virginia suburban sprawl. The hour was so late it was actually the morning after election day. Our newly elected governor's team had planned the order of show with my team.

You will speak for a certain amount of time.

You'll move to stage right.

The governor will follow.

What do you want for your entrance music?

Yes, we'll cue it up.

They were very professional. Extremely organized.

But it's election night! Nothing goes as planned. You can throw the script away because that crowd is going to take you where it takes you.

I gazed out at those gathered. The room was packed, and then in the back was a large riser jampacked with cameras. The media was out in force tonight. Most of them had probably thought they were going to broadcast a series of concession speeches, since the governor and I are elected separately, but we were about to give them a different story.

"I am at a loss for words—for the first time in my life," I began.

"We love you," called a female voice from the crowd.

"I love you, too." I raised my arms in the air trying to hug the crowd somehow in a metaphoric way, or at least show my equal excitement.

"Oorah!" a male voice shouted. My husband, Terry, who was

standing beside me, echoed it. I recognized the meaning of the shout immediately, of course, and up went one of my fists to bump the air.

"Oorah!" I called back. "Marine Corps!" More cheers from the crowd. "Motivated! Dedicated!"

Then it was time to get back to the task at hand. I was standing on this stage for a victory speech. I had on this evening been elected the lieutenant governor of the Commonwealth of Virginia in the good, old U.S.A. It was a night of firsts. I was Virginia's first female lieutenant governor. I was the first *Black* female elected statewide. I was the first female immigrant lieutenant governor. I was the first female veteran. But as much as I appreciated achieving these milestones in my home state—my chosen and much-beloved Commonwealth—I was not here to exult in accomplishments. I was not on that stage for me.

I was on the stage first for God, for the Lord and Savior who had guided me for so long, shored me up, shown me the way, answered so many prayers, given me the occasional sign, and, just as importantly, had told me, "No, child"—"no" in the most certain, undeniable manner. I was here for my God, and because of my God first and foremost.

But I was also here for the people of Virginia. You see, I had not been elected to be the lieutenant governor of the Republicans in Virginia, of the Independents and Democrats who had voted for me. No, I had been elected to be the lieutenant governor for *all* Virginians. My two reasons for being on the stage were joined hand in hand.

I had been presented with victory by the Lord so that I could assume that responsibility. That was what *He* required of *me*. Nothing less than my best for the people I was elected to represent.

Virginia has the oldest legislature in the New World. It is the birthplace of George Washington. James Madison put forward the Bill of Rights based on the *Virginia* constitution. Virginia had also been a slave state. Yet here I was, a Black woman elected to be second in command in the former capital of the Confederacy, and an immigrant at that. Washington, Jefferson, and Madison might not have envisioned this could happen—but I think they did. Those documents they left behind proclaim as much. The Constitution, conceived and shepherded by a Virginia boy. The Declaration of Independence, written by a Virginia boy. The father of our nation, a Virginia boy.

I am proud to stand among them.

I am a Virginian.

"I'm here because of you, Virginia," I continued. "I'm here because you put your trust in me. That's the only reason I'm here. Thank you! Thank you!"

I took a folded piece of paper from where I'd stashed it under the red dress jacket I was wearing. I opened up the paper. "Got my speech!"

The truth was, there was not much written on the paper my friend had thrust into my hand and on which I'd scribbled notes. I hadn't planned on this. After all the effort, all the trials, all the hope, the truth was that I had not expected to win. Yet, I also didn't expect to lose.

I knew that this was the first time many who were watching would have seen me or had any idea who I was or where I'd come from. Standing alongside me were the dearest people in my life—people who sustained me and helped make me who I am. Of course, I wanted to talk about them first.

"Let me introduce the people behind me. I've got my husband, Terence. He's another Marine." More cheers from the crowd at this. I gestured to my right. "My daughter Katia." I nodded to my left. "And my other daughter, Janel." My girls smiled and waved.

"I'm telling you that what you're looking at is the American Dream." I repeated the point. "The American Dream."

Cheers and oorahs. I let the uproar die down a bit and continued.

"When my father came to this country August eleventh of 1963, he came from Jamaica at the height of the U.S. civil rights movement. He came—and it was such a bad time for us—but I asked him 'Why did you come?' and he answered that he came because America was where the jobs and the opportunity were. And he only came with a dollar seventy-five. One dollar and seventy-five cents. He took any job he could find, and he put himself through school and started his American Dream. Now he's comfortably retired.

"Then he came and got me when I was six years old. And when I stepped on that Pan-Am Boeing 727 and landed at JFK, I landed in a new world. So let me tell you this: I am not even first-generation American. When I joined the Marine Corps, I was still a Jamaican. But this country had done so much for me that I was willing—willing—to die for this country." Behind me, I knew Terry would be nodding in agreement to this. He felt the same. I raised my right arm.

"U.S.A.!" I called out. It only took that one prompt for the crowd to join in.

"U.S.A.! U.S.A.!"

I couldn't help myself, but gesticulated to them like an ecstatic minister of music or orchestra director. There was no need to do this, of course. They were already in perfect harmony, and the chants were music uniting us all. This went on for a while until I had to signal I needed to go on. After all, the governor had yet to speak! I began to feel the tick of the clock, and that weight of responsibility mixed with deep gratitude returned, as well.

"And so I say to you...victory, indeed, yes. But I say to you, there are some who want to divide us and we must not let that happen. They would like us to believe we are back in 1963 when my father came. But we can live where we want. We can eat where we want. We *own* the water fountains. We have had a Black president elected not once, but twice, and here I am, living proof! In case you haven't noticed, I am Black, and I have been Black all my life. But that's not what this is about. We are going to be about the business of the Commonwealth. We have things to tend to. We are going to fully fund our historically Black colleges and universities. You're going to hear from your governor-elect, Glenn Youngkin, and he's got a day-one plan that I'm already tired about."

This may have sounded a bit confusing, but I'd momentarily reflected what we were dedicated to accomplishing. It was quite a list. The people of Virginia were counting on us to implement it. "Don't know how we're going to make it to day two.

"But he's going to make sure we keep more of our money in our pockets, because he's going to get rid of all kinds of taxes. We're going to have safer neighborhoods, safer communities." I raised a fist in emphasis, talking about the issue closest to my heart. "And our children are going to get a good education! Because education lifted my father out of poverty. Education lifted me out of poverty. Education will lift us all out of poverty because we must have marketable skills so that our children can not only survive, but they will thrive. They will create generational wealth. That's what this is about."

More calls of excitement and appreciation from the gathered crowd.

"It's a historic night. Yes, it is. But I didn't run to make history. I just wanted to leave it better than I found it. And with your help, we're going to do that. We're going to have transparent government. And as I used to say when we were on the trail, hold on Virginia, help is on the way! The cavalry has arrived!"

More cheers.

"Thank you. God bless you! And finally..."

"Winsome! Winsome! Winsome!" the crowd called out. This was getting a bit embarrassing, and the governor needed to make his announcement. Time to wind it up!

"Want to thank my staff, because I couldn't have done it without them. We were a rag-tag bunch of people. We ran an impossible, improbable campaign..."

"God was with us," someone shouted from the audience.

"God was exactly with us, otherwise we would never have made it."

I gestured upward with my open palm. "And so I want to finish up by thanking you, Jesus!"

I finished with what had become not merely my slogan, the slogan of my campaign staff, but of this extraordinary election filled with echoes that would reverberate throughout America in the coming years. The back of the room was filled with a veritable bandstand of national media aiming their cameras and microphones toward me. We had fought back and won against a dark shadow that had covered our Commonwealth. It was a Goliath of idiotic politics, of insane school policies that sought to indoctrinate children in family-destroying propaganda, and the collapse of education due to institutions exercising raw and corrupt power during a nationwide pandemic. Virginia could indeed be a harbinger for change in America. We were David going up against Goliath. I was aware of it. Governor-elect Youngkin knew it, too. Our newly elected attorney general knew it. We'd felt it in the campaign as a rising tide turning our dim prospects first into hope, and then into determined certainty. Virginia had elected us because the Commonwealth needed saving. No wonder I felt such responsibility.

But tonight was for celebrating, for catching our breath to take on the challenges ahead. Tonight was victory against opponents with ludicrously high amounts of funding, with a tremendous assortment of institutions backing them. Tonight was victory against all odds. So I cried out with joy the feeling that rose in my heart.

"How sweet it is!"

Chapter One

JAMAICA BABY

"There's going to be a tug-of-war for this child."

These were the prophetic words of Alberta Campbell, my great-grandmother, my mother's grandmother. The child she was talking about was me.

This is not an unusual problem in Jamaica, the country of my birth. I was born in Kingston, the capital city, and largest town on the island. My mom and dad were neighbors. My mother's name is Olive Harris, but everyone calls her Sweetie. My father is William Earle. Everyone calls him Willie. Both are still alive, my mother in Jamaica, my father in retirement in Georgia.

They lived nearby and grew up around one another. My dad's family was much richer than Mom's family—rich for third world Jamaica in the 1950s and early 1960s, that is.

My mother and father grew up together. Because of me they have remained connected for life. My father later married (and divorced). I have a sister as a result. My mother never did marry.

I was born March 11, 1964.

My mother's family had not started off poor. Alberta's father had worked as a plantation overseer in Jamaica. He had received some education. She was the only child and inherited quite a bit of money when he died, as well as property all over the island. She even had one of the first cars in Jamaica.

Alas, great-grandmother Alberta lost it all. She lost most of it through terrible deals and investments. They had enough to get by on, but the go-go time of my great-grandmother's youth was past. She and her children ended up living on one remaining property, which they'd transformed into a residence. This is where my mother lives to this day. It's about two acres, with lots of tropical fruit trees, and my grandmother grew grapes, as well.

By the time my mother came along, her family had grown quite poor. My father was leaving for America. He emigrated in August 1963.

My maternal grandmother, Sylvia Harris; my grandfather, William Harris.

In those days, the great Jamaican migration to America had just begun. In generations prior, most emigrating Jamaicans would go to England. When my father flew to America, he went on a British passport. It listed him as born in the "British West Indies." Jamaica had become an independent country in 1962, but it was still part of the British Commonwealth.

My mother and father were never married. Yet, as we will see, my father in no way abandoned me, and neither did my mother, of course.

My mother named me Winsome. It's an uncommon English girl's name. Since William Earle is my dad, my maiden name is Winsome Earle.

When Dad came to New York in 1963, he arrived with nothing but $1.75 in his pocket. But he had high hopes and an indomitable will to make a life for himself in this new country. Dad lived with his older sister, who had immigrated to the Bronx. He worked all manner of jobs to get started, really anything he could get. There was no way he could allow himself to fail. My grandparents would have been ashamed. His family would have been mortified. People would say, "Willie went to big-big America and did nothing? Worthless!" He had gotten the opportunity that other people did not. He knew he *had* to do well. He must do well. Everything had already been arranged for my father to go. There were great expectations and great pressure for success in America.

Fortunately, he had a sound high school education and a plan. He had come with the beginnings of a trade, following in the footsteps of his father. He took classes to get the necessary qualifications for America.

Within a few years, he'd done it. He landed a job as a mechanic and welder working for Pan Am, at the time the greatest airline in the world and America's flag carrier airline to the nations. Dad worked at the recently renamed John F. Kennedy International Airport. He wore coveralls at work—I seem to remember white ones—because he was a welder and a mechanic. His task was the repair and maintenance of the jet engines at JFK. This was back when Pan Am was *the* Pan Am, the airline with moxie.

He worked for Pan Am for decades. And, as a Pan Am employee, he was eligible to purchase discount tickets.

Pan Am flights would soon play prominently in my childhood.

Once I was born Mom came and introduced herself to the Earle family. She also introduced me. My father had grown up very loved in the Earle household. He had been the last born, the baby, and all agreed he was the favorite child. I'm told that as a baby I looked just like him.

I was very sickly as a baby. I wasn't eating anything, and whenever I did eat, I threw it up. My mother and my grandmothers took me to every doctor they could find. Not one could figure out what was wrong. I was at death's door.

My paternal grandmother, however, was not going to give up. She heard about "a woman." We're Christian folks, so to us that meant a spiritual prophet, a person with a divine gift of healing. Well, this woman diagnosed the problem as teething causing excessive swallowing of saliva leading to a bloated stomach. She picked herbs from her backyard—well, she picked leaves from some bush, I never learned what it was—and mixed up a tea. I drank it, and voilà, here I am today.

I don't come from give-up-type people. It's no surprise that my paternal grandmother was the one who found the woman who saved me. She loved me fiercely.

My father's mother, who was to be instrumental in my life, is named Valda Earle. She was married to Gilbert Earle, my grandfather. He was a mechanic for the then-national bus company, Jamaica Omnibus Services (JOS).

My grandmother took to me instantly. My mother continued to visit, and my grandmother Earle began to babysit me. By that time, my mother had found a job at a manufacturing plant. She worked there for years and eventually became a junior executive. At the time, she worked on the factory floor and had to be absent for long hours during her shift.

At that time in Jamaica, grandmothers ran the show. I think it comes from African roots. Grandmother Valda kept asking for me and asking for me. She'd send my grandfather with the car if need be.

Eventually my father's parents invited my mom to move in. So my mother stayed with my dad's parents part of the time and her own family at other times. Valda would keep sending my grandfather to come and pick me up when we were away with my mom's family. With my mother's new job, it was a very good arrangement.

This was when Alberta, my great-grandmother, said to my mother, "There's going to be a tug-of-war for this child." She added, "And anyway, the Earles can provide more opportunities for the child. Let her go and live with her father's people."

So my mother went to live with my father's mother and father fully. This is not so unusual in Jamaica. It's accepted as one of the things families might do. There are many cousins living together with the grandparents or with other relatives. Everybody's going away to

America, to Canada, or to England. If you go abroad, you work until you can afford to send for the rest of the family to join you. In fact, many of my Earle and Harris uncles and aunts had immigrated either to America or England. My uncle, my father's older brother, and his wife had also moved to America. They had left their two children with my grandmother until they could bring them.

That was how I moved into my grandmother Valda's house, my childhood home. My father was not always absent, but came back regularly. He would make a long visit from New York every year. My earliest memory of him comes from when I was probably three. I was standing near almond trees, all growing in a row. I can still see the blossoms, and he was there with me.

My father seemed like a giant whenever he was around, even though he is only about five foot nine. He sent money to support my mother and me, but my mother banked it for me to have later. Also at the time, believe it or not, Jamaican money—based on the British pound sterling—was worth more than American money. My mother worked at the factory of a company called Metal Box Jamaica. They made tin containers for all sorts of items and uses. She had been promoted to line supervisor by then. She was doing fine in her new job and was able to make ends meet.

When he came to Jamaica, Dad would bring things back for me. My mother had family already in England. She might have gone to England herself, but she never wanted to immigrate there, and then, of course, she had me. Her family in England would send things for me, as well.

I was the new baby. I got toys, and later books and school items, from my father, and shoes and clothes from England. My mom got along well with Valda. The two women liked one another. It was agreed that I would, at least as a toddler, permanently live at my grandmother's.

Many times later in life I asked my mother, "Why did you let this tug-of-war continue? Why didn't you tell my grandmother that I'm your child and I was staying with you?" But down deep I have always understood. My mom did what was best for me at the time.

This arrangement meant that my grandmother had the most say over me. I fell asleep in my bed in her house. I woke up with the Jamaican sun shining through the jalousie windows of the room I shared with my cousin. My grandmother dressed me. She fed me. She played with me. She disciplined me when necessary. She was, for all intents and purposes, my second mother.

This was reflected in what we all called her.

We called her "Mommy."

My mother was "Mom," and my grandmother was "Mommy."

Of course, my maternal grandparents were also in my life, as well. I was a very loved child and grandchild. My mother eventually moved back in with her parents. She was much closer to her workplace there, and she knew she was leaving me in good hands. It was as my great-grandmother had said, and her advice had helped them avoid the worst tug-of-war. I lived at the Earles'.

My grandparents didn't have a phone, and neither did my mother. The neighbors did have a phone, however, and my grandmother could reach my mother at work if necessary

At times my mother kept me for longer periods. When I was with my mother, I had my own room, but it was small, kind of a cubby. Most of the time, I slept with her. I loved that. I got to be hugged in bed. Often she'd come and get me on the weekends, and then I'd go visit her side of the family, which was also very big. I got to know all those cousins. She lived about three miles away. It was a bus ride away, but you could also walk, which we frequently did.

My mother always wore gold bangles—ten or more gold bangles on each arm. I would hear the gold bangles and I would get so excited. My mother is here! But sometimes it was my grandmother, who also jingled when she walked. My heart would fall; it wasn't my mother.

At this time, most women wore gold bangles in Jamaica. This may have arisen from the East Indian influence. And you never had just *one*. You had five or six at minimum. You got them from the Indian jewelers, and they didn't buy them from suppliers; they made them.

I had gold bangles as a baby, as well. All girl babies did. Mine were adjustable as I grew. I had two bangles, a ring, and gold earrings. Girl babies must have earrings! You're a bad parent if your baby girl doesn't. It's a cultural thing.

But I always came back to my grandmother's. The arrangement made sense. At my mother's, I had to wake up very early; she had to take me to school then take a long ride back to work.

So I saw her frequently, and I often stayed weekends at her place. It did not seem an unusual or stressful existence to me as a toddler. I had no other life with which to compare it. I missed my mother when she was not there. I sometimes longed for her greatly. But I wasn't traumatized. Instead, I felt surrounded by love.

*   *   *

My early childhood in Jamaica was blissful. My grandmother's house was a sort of little Eden. The house was set quite far from the road. In fact, it was barely in shouting distance. We lived in the Oakland Crescent area. Many Kingston neighborhoods at that time were like the American suburbs in that they had yards. Our house was built in the center of around three acres. What took up most of that space?

Fruit trees.

There was every kind of fruit tree you could think of. They bore fruit throughout the year. You never could truly go hungry. We were surrounded by superfood, as we might call it now. An American apple has many vitamins and minerals, but a mango has more than double that. We had avocado trees. We had tamarind trees. We had cocoa; we could make natural hot chocolate from the tree and cocoa butter you could skim.

Grass had grown in most parts of the yard. Under the trees, the ground was dirt in spots, gravel in others, however, it was often covered, since there were so many fruit trees and the leaves were constantly falling off. One of my poor cousins would be tasked with raking the yard, and it was a never-ending undertaking. When I was old enough, that became one of my chores, as well.

My grandmother's fruit trees always produced something, no matter what time of year it was. Jamaica is hot. The sun shines most of the time, although there are storms, and sometimes hurricanes. You can think of the seasons as dry and wet. A better way to measure them might be by what type of fresh fruit is available. Jamaica is near the equator. Kingston is on a parallel with Belize, southern Mexico, and Guatemala. The average annual temperature is around eighty-five degrees.

We ate fruit all the time, depending on what was in season. I think we had three or four types of mango trees, one of our favorite fruits, and they would bear at different times. Some kinds of mangos were more valuable and tastier than others. You could sell an East Indian mango, one of the best kinds, for what would have been around seven dollars in today's money.

How do you tell a ripe mango? Sometimes when it turns yellow. This depends on the species, however. Most of the time, you just push on it. If it gives a little, then you know it's ready. But if you eat it and it's not quite ready, then it'll really do a number on your stomach. Be careful with that.

Our house, as with most houses in Kingston, was surrounded by a fence. Especially along the front, this was more a civilized barrier than some impassible obstruction. People might open your gate, or find some other way through or over, and pick your mangos to eat or sell. Pilfering mangos was not exactly a nefarious crime—they're just mangos, after all—but you didn't want to lose *all* of them to poachers.

Mangos were great, but the crown jewels of the yard were the ackee trees. We had two. In Jamaica, you must have an ackee tree. Almost every home has at least one. It's the national fruit and part of the national dish, ackee and salt fish. To tell the truth, I don't know what ackee is in a horticultural sense, but we ate a *lot* of it.

Ackee trees bear four times a year. You must be careful about picking them. If you don't allow the fruit to naturally open after ripening but attempt to force them open, the fruit will poison you. You will become very, very sick, and possibly die. Once the pod ripens, you boil the inner meat and fry it with salt fish. Salt fish is just heavily salted fish, but we call it salt fish in Jamaica.

How do you avoid poisoning yourself and obtain fresh ackee? Ackee comes in a red pod with a star shape. One will fit into the palm of your hand. You *must* wait for it to open. It truly is poisonous before that. When it opens, inside is the fruit. There are usually three fruit structures in an ackee pod. You will find three clumps of yellow flesh with three big black seeds attached.

You pick the pod from the tree, then you sit down with your ackees and process them. Jamaicans can do this with great adroitness. You pull them all the way open, then reach in and pluck out the yellowish fruit clumps. You remove the big black seeds and the pink fibers that hold the seeds in place.

There, attached to the inside of the pod, is fruit. This crinkled yellow fruit, cleaned of seeds and pink flesh, is what you eat. You boil it. To finish the meal you soak the salt fish to remove most of the salt. Then you put everything into a Dutch pot and cook it further. Cooked ackee takes on the texture of scrambled eggs. About two dozen ackee pods will make a family meal for four or five. By the way, Jamaicans use the traditional "Dutch pot"—imported long, long ago from Holland, and nowadays made of cast aluminum—as our primary cooking pot.

You also combine ackee and salt fish with breadfruit, plantains (we pronounce it "PLAN-tins"), and green bananas (a specific variety used for cooking). You boil it together with the green bananas, a dumpling or two, and you have the main meal on a Sunday.

I'm not an expert cook, Jamaican or otherwise, but my very American family will have it on occasion. If you're going to be very extravagant, instead of salt fish, you might use bacon. In my childhood, using bacon would mean that you had money! We generally stuck with the traditional salt fish, however. And you must have freshly squeezed orange juice to accompany your ackee and salt fish. Now that's a meal! That'll take you through a whole Sunday.

I have to confess: My husband doesn't like ackee and salt fish. That's okay; more for us! All that a Jamaican American has to say is, "Hey, I have some fresh ackee," and everyone else wants to know when they can get some. When my mother comes to America she will often bring a bag of ackee fruit. Yes, you can buy ackee in a can at a Jamaican food store, but it's not the same. It's not the fresh, wonderful ackee of my childhood, but it will do!

The tamarind trees in my maternal grandparents' yard were descendants of the original stock that had been brought to the island when the Indians—or, as we called them, East Indians—migrated from India. The Chinese brought fruit and vegetables, too, notably bok choi. We called it "pop chow" in Jamaica. The plantains came from Africa. We had guavas native to Jamaica when I was young, but those got wiped out for some reason. The guavas on the island now come from somewhere else.

We also had a coconut tree. We call the produce of the tree "water coconut." You could either pick them early—"young coconuts," we called those—and the flesh would be jellylike, or you could let them continue to grow and the coconut would become like you see in America. After you take off the husk, you have the brown shell. Inside is coconut milk, but we never drank the milk. Instead, we used the milk as a stock for another favorite dish of Jamaica: rice and peas. You would think of rice and peas in America as rice and red beans, but we called beans peas. Rice and peas is always served very well seasoned, of course.

We would also make coconut oil from the milk. And for a final use, we'd skim off the cream when we juiced coconuts and use it to make another signature dish of Jamaica, rundown. Rundown is made with mackerel, a fish that was also considered extravagant, like bacon. Rundown was a special meal.

These dishes sound exotic, but they were what we ate when I was a child. I can't make them. I'm only now learning how to cook rice and peas properly. The truth is, I never really learned the ins and outs. I was always the youngest and my older cousins did the cooking. I still can't make a proper dumpling, which is a travesty. But there it is. You can boil or fry dumplings. I like flour dumplings. Corn dumplings I've always hated.

Speaking of corn, Jamaican babies get cornmeal porridge. I certainly did. Eating baby porridge is one of my earliest memories. This is Jamaican baby food, and I certainly got my share. It's served well seasoned. There's cinnamon in it, plus nutmeg, vanilla, and bay leaf, which gives it an aromatic flavor, all mixed in condensed milk. Pimento, another seasoning, goes with cornmeal, and it's in the baby porridge, as well. I made porridge for my children when they were young, and they loved it. Here in America, I used cream of wheat and seasoned it Jamaican style. Corn porridge is delicious. Even when we were older, we would eat this from time to time. It must be made from fresh cornmeal, not store-bought. How do you make it? You put the corn in the pestle and you grind it, that's how!

The odor of Jamaican cooking always takes me back, as aromas usually do for anyone who has come from another country, another culture. There were often delicious odors in my grandmother's house. Saturday was the time for chicken soup. There was a chicken foot in it. I wouldn't (and still won't) eat chicken foot. There's thyme in the soup, as well. You can tell when thyme is in a meal. It's a hearty, tasty soup. Our soups are chock-full of seasoning.

In Jamaica, you don't use a lot of salt because the herbs give it so much flavor it wakens up the meat and other ingredients. On Sundays another typical meal might be curry goat and white rice. This is served with plantains and callaloo. Callaloo is a Jamaican amaranth. It's part of the spinach family, like collards, but there's no bitterness to it. It's made with coconut oil, onions, and garlic.

Tropical spice and seasoning transform everything in Jamaica. When Irish immigrants first came to Jamaica, they didn't season their food so much, but Jamaica had its influence over time. Now Jamaican corn beef and cabbage is highly seasoned, much more so than in Ireland. I ordered some at an Irish pub here in America, and it was so blah. Not even onion? Not even black pepper? Just the beef? Our corn beef and cabbage in Jamaica is fabulous.

Jamaican food is very peppery, too. It's filled with lots of Scotch Bonnet peppers, the pepper Mexicans call habanero. They're not simply hot, they're also flavorful. Everybody eats Scotch Bonnets; you grow up with the taste.

As I said, I never did much cooking. I was among the babies. My older cousins or my grandmother, aunt, or mom would cook. In America, my dad would cook. He cooked Jamaican and American food. He still loves to cook.

When I was first with my husband and I would make dinner, I said to him, "Share the dinner."

He replied, "What does that even mean?"

I answered, "It means take some of the food and put it on the plate." It's the Jamaican way of saying this.

My husband says, "We call that 'serving.'" Well, our belief is that we "share" our meals.

If a neighbor drops by and we know they don't have much to eat, we'll say "share a plate for Mr. So-and-so, Mrs. So-and-so." Share a plate for them and take it to them later.

Other things seemed very strange in America to me at first. In Jamaica, we never had mayonnaise—our idea of a spread was gravy.

It was also not unusual to have dinner for breakfast. You might have ribs for breakfast, left over from the night before. I still do this. My husband, who is so American, looks at me and shakes his head sometimes. In America, breakfast food is supposed to be distinct and different!

When I was a child, I drank hot English tea constantly. Everyone drank English tea, and only the adults drank coffee. We had tea in the afternoons, tea to go to bed. Even now my husband asks me how I can drink tea or coffee right before bed. That was how I was raised.

When I almost died as a baby, the natural healer had gathered leaves from...some bush. That's the way the island is. It seems to sprout healthy and medicinal plants in every backyard.

Whatever that bush was, they boiled its leaves, and here I am. During my early, growing up years, only when someone was ill did we normally drink so many of the herbal teas we've come to know now. A trip to the doctor was mostly unheard of, since there was some kind of medicinal bush in the backyard or in the market to alleviate illness.

I can remember that though we had toothbrushes, I saw others use a special twig as a toothbrush—knowledge passed down by our elders. We are losing that knowledge.

Chapter Two

MOMMY'S HOUSE

When people hear me talk about coming to America as a child it can sound complicated, and it was. Sometimes I refer to arriving in America at the age of six, and sometimes at the age of twelve. The truth is, both are accurate. I went to live with my father until I was nine in New York, with summers and holidays in Jamaica. I returned to living in Jamaica and my grandmother's house for three years, then moved back to America permanently when I was almost thirteen. So my Jamaican childhood was interspersed with the portion of my childhood spent in the Bronx. In my memory, the two are intimately mixed.

My father is about five foot nine. My mother is about five foot three. I ended up somewhere in between at about five four and a half. My dad is a bit light-skinned; he's got curly hair. His father's mother, Sarah, was a green-eyed White woman from Ireland who married my great-grandfather, Robert, a very dark-skinned man. His father, my grandfather Gilbert, was light-skinned with wiry hair. My father's mother, my grandmother Valda, was also mixed. Her mother was dark complexioned, but Valda's father was White. We're a typical Jamaican mix.

My family was well respected. We did have "a few shillings," as the saying goes. We were not poor, but we were certainly not well-to-do. Both sides of my family rose from nothing to property owners—education did that. My grandmother's house did not have air-conditioning. Most people didn't have it in Jamaica. Only the very wealthy did back then.

Because my grandfather was a mechanic for the bus company and could easily keep it up, we had a car. Most people didn't. My grandparents owned their property. Even though she'd only had an eighth-grade education, my grandmother was very intelligent and was very shrewd with money. She spoke very well. She wrote well. She was a voracious reader.

Mommy's mother had been very dark-skinned. Her father, we believe, was a Jewish man. My grandmother had light skin and straighter, wavy hair. I remember asking her about that when I was a child, and she answered, "Well, it's because my father was an East Indian." But we think he was Jewish. One day we'll sort it out.

In Jamaica, as in many Caribbean islands that were part of the British Empire, there are many East Indians whose families migrated from India, often in the 1800s. But my daughter has turned up quite a bit doing genealogical research and having our DNA analyzed. We believe my great-grandfather might have been of Syrian or Sephardic Jewish origin. There has long been a Jewish community on the island founded by a man named Abraham Cohen Henriques in 1670. Henriques came fleeing the Spanish Inquisition. Also Jewish settlers might have come with Christopher Columbus on his second voyage. There was an established Jewish community by the time the English captured Jamaica from the Spaniards.

*   *   *

Gilbert Earle, my paternal grandfather and Valda's husband, was very tall. He was light-skinned. As I've said, his father was a dark-skinned man who had married an Irish woman. One thing that impressed me as a child were his very long, straight legs.

My grandmother became my world, but my grandfather was more

of a mystery to me. I never got to know him the way my cousins got to know him. He loved me as a baby, but after I went away, he grew more reserved. He was always a quiet man. My grandmother was a vocal, determined woman. She made up for his reserve with her outgoing nature. My grandfather was well spoken. He spoke a British type of English, and seldom used Jamaican patois.

I believe my grandfather suffered from lifelong PTSD. He'd been in World War II. At the time, they called it shell shock. You were just expected to get over it—except he didn't. His way of dealing with it was, from time to time, drinking rum to relieve himself of whatever horrors had resurfaced. Barely twenty years had passed since World War II, after all. He would never talk about the war except when he was drunk or tipsy. Then we grandchildren would listen intently because he would say things he never otherwise revealed.

I remember one of the things he would say is "Churchill killed the Germans like rats." He would tell us about U-boats and the barrels of oil in the sea, and other experiences. It may be strange to say, but my love of history comes from him. I've always had a particular interest in and reverence for British prime minister Winston Churchill because my grandfather brought him to life! Other than those rare war reminiscences, my grandfather didn't say much.

Gilbert and Valda had saved up enough money to buy another piece of property, and at the time they rented that property out. They had built a duplex there, and eventually built even more houses on the property. They had made enough so that they could send my aunt to England to nursing school where she had a scholarship, and my father and his brother to America. They did not have enough money to support the sons once they were abroad. On the contrary, they were expected to work and send money back—hence my father arriving with $1.75 in his pocket.

My father's sister, Aunt Violet, returned from England in my later childhood and helped raise me. She was an RN, whereas most other nurses in Kingston hospitals would have been something lesser than an RN. We called her Aunt Babs.

By the way, in Jamaica our nicknames are never anything close to what our true names are. Often, people do not know our true names until we're dead and they see the name on the grave marker. For example, I have a cousin whom I thought was named Colleen. Then one day when I was about eighteen, I saw her with an initial ring. On it was etched "ME."

"Who is ME?" I asked her. "It should be 'CE' for Colleen Earle.'"

She replied, "My real name is Marlene."

How did she become Colleen? I don't know. It can seem arbitrary. When we send Christmas cards among Jamaicans and Jamaican Americans, we'll sometimes put in parentheses what our nickname is so the recipient knows who sent it. So Aunt Violet was Aunt Babs. I mean, "Babs" is supposed to be short for "Barbara," right?

* * *

Aunt Babs was the third extremely important matriarchal figure in my youth. Aunt Babs was a thoroughly modern 1970s woman back then. She wore an afro. She had returned from England to become the head operating theatre nurse at a hospital. In America, you might call her a head OR nurse. She trained other nurses as well. You could tell she'd been to England by her manner of speaking, lots of Britishisms. Like the traditional British nurses, she did not wear her nurse uniform outside of the hospital. Even without it, she always carried herself a different way. You *knew* she was a woman cut from very different cloth.

This was Jamaica, so we did not pronounce "Babs" with a short "a" sound, but rather with an "ah" vowel sound, so that it comes out as something like Aunt "Bobs" or "Bahbs," an even stranger diminutive of her full name, Violet Earle Dexter.

Which brings me to the subject of the Jamaican manner of speaking. We spoke two languages everywhere, standard British English and Jamaican broken English, or patois. Now in Jamaica, you're not supposed to speak patois to strangers. Furthermore, if you speak broken English all the time, you're looked down upon as less educated. Now it's not so much that way, but back then that's how it was.

We weren't allowed to speak patois at home. You could speak it with your friends, but you couldn't speak it generally as a rule. People would correct you immediately.

Jamaican standard English pronunciations were much more English than American. For example, if I were to speak to you in that way, you might hear it as a cross between the queen of England and the type of Jamaican accent one hears today. There was a lot of British in it. My grandfather Gilbert was a very formal speaker in this manner. He would say "GA-rahj" for "garage" instead of the American "guh-RAHJ," and so forth.

I speak Jamaican patois perfectly well, of course. I have kept in practice by years of speaking with my family! When I talk with my mother, I don't speak deep patois, as it is called. To speak broken English was a sign of disrespect when I was growing up. Nowadays in Jamaica, everything in the class structure as reflected by the language has changed. This is a different generation. The old ways aren't the new ways, I guess. But sure, I speak patois.

My husband, Terry, has been many times to Jamaica. He tries to speak patois down there at times. We natives laugh at him; he's so clearly an American. I'm sure you've watched movies where they've supposedly cast someone who allegedly speaks with a Jamaican accent. Let me tell you, that is frequently baloney. Either they've hired some-one from another Caribbean island or country or an American actor attempting to fake it. I can tell someone with a Trinidadian accent from someone from Haiti, Guyana, or Barbados instantly.

Incidentally, my cousins who came to America very young? Well, they were socialized here. When they try to speak patois, yes, they're a little better than my husband—but they all have American accents!

*   *   *

Although we were surrounded by a big yard with fruit trees, the neighborhood of Oakland Crescent was well within the city. The house was concrete block. Most of the houses in Jamaica are block construction. Perhaps it's to withstand hurricanes.

Concrete construction is hot as the dickens in warm weather. They retain the heat of the day into the hot afternoon when you need to be cool. Fans were constantly whirring inside, but we spent a great deal of our time on the veranda. Back in those days, the veranda surrounded the house like an extended patio, and all sides were open. There weren't railings or barriers.

With the result of the crimes that followed the political unrest starting in the early 1970s, people began putting up burglar bars around homes to prevent break-ins. These were often beautiful wrought iron creations. But the whole veranda, instead of being open, became closed in. That's what you see today. The residents are used to them now, but verandas weren't always that way. Now even if you live in areas that are not prone to crime, people usually have burglar bars anyway. It's a security feature, and has become part of the culture.

Even with the bars, people practically live outside on their verandas much of the time. We certainly did at my grandmother's house. The porch furniture was either wicker or wrought iron, sometimes a wooden chair. Think tropical! The cushions were of print fabric, the motif always lush and colorful.

The yard was huge. This was typical of many houses in the neighborhood. The driveway was very long. The front fence line matches the house. It's a concrete fence that is primarily decorative. Most have a flat, even surface, and are about four feet in height. To prevent young men from sitting on fences, people sometimes set them with spikes along the top to keep them clear—either you build a high enough fence, or you put in the spikes. Some people didn't have spiked front fences, but we did at my grandmother's.

The original house was just two bedrooms, one bath. Big enough, with the kitchen and living and dining room. Once the kids went off to America and England, they sent money back and expanded the house. Over the years, the house underwent a series of renovations. It became bigger, bathrooms were added, and it grew outwardly, with a new section of veranda put in along the larger perimeter.

When you leave Jamaica, you are expected to be successful. Why? Because you've got to help back home. You've received a job, an education. Now you're expected, very nearly required, to provide. So Jamaican immigrants can't afford to come and while away their lives. Some do, sure. But not the vast majority. If they do, the folks back home consider them worthless—and, to tell the truth, so do their relatives in America. You hear it, sometimes in jest, sometimes not. "You're worthless! You're a worthless child, your parents are ashamed of you!"

* * *

As I said, my grandfather had a car, which was very unusual back then. It was a British Austin. We were, after all, a former British colony—and an *actual* British colony for most of my grandfather's youth—so much of what we had was British. When the generation prior to my father's emigrated, they immigrated to England, and many still did. They would send things home from England. My aunt Babs did. So did my mother's family. My shoes were Jumping Jacks, nice leather Clarks. We wore English shoes, English clothes. We often had English-style furniture in the house. We never wanted American things as much as British back then. British items were, well, British. Impeccable.

Once enough people had immigrated to America and Canada, Jamaicans wanted more American goods. British items seemed old-fashioned. American products were modern and efficient. Somehow they even felt different—and better. For example, Dove soap was prized in our household. Boy, my family wasted a lot of water using that soap. The darn stuff has conditioning cream built in, so it feels like you never can wash it off.

Ivory was the soap you sent or brought home as a present for the neighbors. Of course, you had to bring them something. You could never visit Jamaica empty-handed. Everybody *knows* you went to America—so what are you bringing for presents? Even today, when you go back to see family, you've got to throw cans of something or another, or some health and beauty products, in your suitcase. Something with "cashmere" in the name, perhaps. Anything that seems exotic and luxurious. Back then, if you really liked your neighbor, you would bring them Dove soap, like family. If they were just okay people, you would bring Ivory. But you had to bring something!

*   *   *

My grandmother's house was painted orange on the outside. It had blue walls on the inside. The interior walls were the other side of the concrete blocks, coated with plaster. There was no sheetrock. Construction was concrete through and through. On the bottoms of the interior walls, there was brown paint meant to be imitation wainscotting—that is, instead of lining the lower wall with wood board, we used paint. It's hard to put wood on concrete, after all.

You came up the steps to the burglar bars. You unlocked the gate. You stepped onto the veranda and went to the door. This opened into the living room–dining room combination—open concept, as we call it today. Not all Jamaican houses are like this anymore. The old way of making homes in Jamaica has the living room in the front, the dining room behind that, then the kitchen all the way back. On either side there are the bedrooms and bathrooms, a room adjoining each bathroom. Perhaps this mirrors the English way of doing things.

I shared my room with my cousin. She was older than I was by four years. Her father was in America. She and her brother were more like my brother and sister than cousins. She and I slept together on a queen bed when I was little, then when we got older, we each had our own.

We didn't have closets; we had wardrobes. These were wooden wardrobes with mirrors, and these were beautifully carved from mahogany. My grandfather's father had been a cabinetmaker. He had made the wardrobes. He made our davenports and other furniture of mahogany, too.

I used to measure my growth by the big living room davenport. The davenport was a blue-leather and wood couch. It had spindles in the arms. I would put my head up against one end and see if my foot could touch the other end. One day my foot finally touched the other spindles! I felt like such a big girl. Other people use the standing-up method. I measured my growth lying down.

I wish that I had some of that furniture. Mahogany, most of it. Brass handles. Just gorgeous. Each room had its own wardrobe, and we had a double wardrobe, two mirrors on each side with the drawers in the middle and drawers underneath. It was at least six or seven feet tall. I had one side, my cousin the other.

By the bed were side tables with electric fans on them. There were no ceiling fans back then. We had light fixtures in the ceiling.

Our windows were screenless glass jalousies. This is the type you open by turning a crank. They are made of panes of glass, each maybe three inches wide by twenty-four inches long. They're thin. Maybe ten or twenty panes set in a row. You turn the crank and they all open or close together. As Jamaica became more modernized, the jalousies became metal or wooden. I miss those glass windows on the houses.

I did my homework out on the porch or in the dining room. I would sit on the davenport or at the dining room table. It was a huge, round table that probably would cost thousands today. It really was massive. You could sit on its huge, clawed feet, which jutted out. Deep under the table was a good spot for hide-and-seek.

Sometimes when it was very hot, we ate on the veranda on trays, the old food trays with fold-out legs. In Jamaica we ate with knife and fork, and you were expected to use them the right way. When I met my husband, he'd cut with the knife, put it down, then switch his fork to that hand, the knife hand, to eat. So weird! We did it the English way. You continue to hold your knife in your right hand, your fork in the other. I taught my children the English way. Plus, you don't hold the fork like it's a weapon to stab with, and you don't hold it like a pencil, either.

Curtains framed the windows inside. Following Jamaican custom, these curtains stayed up exactly a year, then we got a new set. We also painted the house once a year around Christmas and New Year. There was a garage where my grandfather tinkered and the Austin was kept.

We kept a key in the front door pushed into the inside side of the lock. If you didn't have your key, it was possible to slide a piece of paper under the door, poke through the keyhole with something, and push the key out, then pull it under the door. But as crime became more prevalent, they replaced the lock with a different one, so you couldn't do it anymore.

The doors to the interior rooms had glass knobs, just like you see in the antiques stores these days. I used to think they were so old-fashioned. I wanted nice, glistening metal knobs. Now I miss those glass knobs.

The floors were terrazzo tile. We had white terrazzo in one room, and red, black, and blue in others. When anyone came into the house, they had to take their shoes off. You'd usually have your house slippers waiting for you right at the door. You'd be admonished to keep your feet off the cold tile floor so you wouldn't catch a cold.

Taking off shoes inside the house is common in Jamaica. You don't want to bring in dirt from the streets. Your veranda is tiled, so often you take off your shoes before going on the porch. I do think it's healthier to leave outside shoes by the door. As I grew up in the United States, when you came to my house, you needed to remove your shoes and go in sock feet. I enforced this particularly when I had babies crawling the floor.

My grandmother's place was a one-story house. The roof was zinc. Some Jamaican houses have concrete or terra-cotta tile roofs. My grandfather eventually put in terra-cotta, but when I was young, it was zinc.

I loved to hear the rain on that metal roof. It was music to my ears. I'm a big lover of storms to this day. Even now when it's thundering and lightning, I'll go to the window and stare out. Reminds me of my childhood with the rain beating on those jalousie windows. Rain with thunder and lightning, love it. Rain *without* thunder and lightning? Eh, what's the point?

Because the power was iffy in Jamaica, our lights frequently went out at the slightest puff of storm and wind. We had "Home Sweet Home" hurricane lamps at the ready. These always had "Home Sweet Home" imprinted on the bulbous part of the globe. These are the glass kerosene lamps. You had to have at least two, one for the front of the house and one to walk around with.

Speaking of old-fashioned items, my grandmother had a coal stove out back. One birthday, I believe it was my tenth, my mother was getting ready for my birthday party. Most people were beginning to transition from kerosene stoves to propane, which came in gas cylinders. Normally people had two of those five-foot cylinders, one and a spare. When you started the second one, you made an appointment with the gas man. He might come the day you ask him, and he might not come for a week. Eventually he would get to you.

But that day, my grandmother had somehow let them both run

out. I was distraught. How would she bake my cake, Jamaican rum cake, which I loved?

Well, she went into the back and made a fabulous cake on the coal stove. This was just a metal container that allowed you to cook with fire coals. The cake was fabulous. Don't ask me how she did it. She must have retained the skill from her earlier days of poverty. It smoked and fumed, but Mommy baked three layers of cake on those coals.

* * *

The front fence had spikes set in it to keep passersby from jumping up and sitting there. The back and side stretches of fence were chain-link. We don't generally have open yards in Kingston.

We had an iron gate. The address plate was metal. It was Number Two on the street. Because the gate is so far from the house, you don't open the gate and come to the door. Most people have dogs, and dogs will bite. There is no doorbell.

How do you alert the people at the house that you are here?

You pick up a stone and you knock on the gate. There's usually one lying nearby. It's been left there by the last person who knocked on the gate. You need a good one that will make a loud noise. You knock on the address plate. Incidentally, the numbers and paint are often worn off Jamaican house address plates from being constantly knocked upon with a stone. The owners come to the front of the burglar bars.

"Yes, can I help you? Oh, it's you. Come in!"

Everybody knows who everybody is. Where do the Earles live? Oh, they're at Number Two. Where do the Rowes live? They're at Number Five.

You walk a lot in Jamaica. When big rains come, the streets flood because the drainage system is not so good. The younger children take off their shoes and socks and walk in the flooded streets for fun. Of course, we were told not to do it because you could be cut by broken glass or a rusty can. But it was so much fun! We walked all the way home in that water. We never told anybody, but we did it all the time.

On the right was a tenement yard, a yard with two houses on it that housed two different families. Our rear neighbors were Indians. They had four boys and two girls. They would share their curry goat with us on occasion, and it was *so* good when they made it. I would often hear Indian music playing through my window.

The Jamaica of my childhood was a true melting pot. Its motto: Out of many, one people. This sounds much like the motto of the country to which I would soon be moving: E pluribus unum.

Chapter Three

A NEW YORK AND JAMAICAN EDUCATION

I arrived in America on a Pan Am Boeing jet. I was six years old and coming to live with my father and his wife, Annette. My dad flew down to Kingston and brought three of us back with him. I arrived with my cousins Hugh and Horace. If my father had not been able to get us all discount tickets due to his job working for Pan Am, there's no way this bevy of children could have afforded the trip all at once. When I was about ten or eleven, he came down again and got another group of nieces and nephews to deliver to their parents. Airline tickets used to be quite expensive.

We flew standby. That's how the employee discount works. You take your chances. The Jamaican passengers would be fully dressed. Hat, gloves, formal everything. When you flew on Pan Am, you flew in style. The Americans, on the other hand, were wearing shorts, slip-on shoes, big floppy hats, and halter tops. Now I understand why. They were going on or coming back from vacation. As a girl, I didn't get it. I could just tell the Americans from Jamaicans. I figured crazy Americans always dressed like that on planes.

We Jamaican kids were also dressed to the nines. We girls wore dresses. We each had a straw hat with a big ribbon hanging down the back. Mine was a nice yellow color. Those were the years of Easter bonnets and children wearing hats when they dressed up.

The stewardesses—no one called them flight attendants back then—wore their blue bowler uniform hats and sky-blue uniforms. They even wore gloves. We got a full meal on the flight, including steak and vegetables.

I was very excited, and also filled with trepidation. I'd left my mother and grandmother behind. Even separation of a few months seemed like forever to a six-year-old.

Getting off the plane was traumatic for me. The smells were different. You exited outside, down a staircase. Then once we got into New York proper, I was hit with the complicated fragrance of the city. One odor that instantly takes me back when I encounter something similar is the smell of the leather-and-chrome interior of my father's American car. He drove a red auto. Dad loves red cars. It was red with a black interior and lots of chrome everywhere.

All around me, people were speaking English. That wasn't supposed to be a problem, but it was! They were speaking in a funny, strange way. The music wafting from apartments and car radios was different, although in Jamaica Sunday radio had always been American Country music (deemed godly). There are times now when I hear certain music from, say, the Temptations or from the Supremes, and I am back again at six, seven, eight.

I always picture myself at this age in New York wearing my winter coat and shivering with the cold. I know all my time there was not spent in winter, but that's how I remember it in general. To this day, I hate cold weather.

I particularly hate snow. Don't push me down in it. I don't want to make any snowballs. I don't want to play in it. I don't want to leave the house in it. I just do not. I guess I'm one of those people who actually requires the sun. The term for it is "seasonal affective disorder." I *need* sun. I don't think I could ever move permanently to Alaska. I'll visit in the summertime with the Midnight Sun!

My husband and I are opposites, by the way. He grew up in South

Dakota and doesn't mind the cold one bit. Or the lack of sun. Every-thing needs to be dim in the house. He's Mr. Vampire. He likes dark-ness. I'm the one who lets the sunshine in. He loves the frosty winters of the Shenandoah Valley. I can take 'em or leave 'em. Over the years, we've arrived at a happy medium.

It doesn't snow in Jamaica. Every now and then, you'll see a dusting on Blue Mountain Peak, which stands over Kingston. That mountain incidentally, gives its name to Jamaican Blue Mountain Peak coffee, which is our brand at home.

I was moving in with my father and his wife, Annette. I knew Annette already. She had come back to Jamaica with him to visit before. She and I got along very well. So everyone in Jamaica knew her when they sent me to New York. There was no bitterness. Everyone had moved on.

In their Bronx apartment, I had my own room. A toddler was also living in the apartment This was my baby sister, Karen. I'm four years older than she is. She was the only child for my father and Annette.

My father decided it was time for me to come. My mother was opposed at first. She was afraid that if I went to America, she would never see me again and I would forget her. My great-grandmother Alberta stepped in yet again and said, "Let the child go to America because there are more opportunities there. And a child cannot for-get her own mother." My mom listened to her grandmother, and off I went.

It was a different time then. Nobody asked me what I wanted. I was a child. Children in those days were to be seen and not heard. We had a different culture in Jamaica, where children were especially to be seen and not heard most of the time. You do what your family tells you to do.

My father's marriage to Annette had also been a factor. I don't think he could have brought me up as a single man. This was another reason my mother worried I would forget her. But the marriage ultimately did not last. She was from Georgia, and had come to New York with her family as part of the great migration of Black people from the South looking for a better life.

She was not a terrible stepmother at all. I loved her very much. She was good to me, and quite loving in return.

My mother tells me that when I came back to Jamaica, I had indeed forgotten her. My grandmother had brought me back to Jamaica. After we arrived, I clung to her and refused to go to my mother.

My grandmother chastised me and said, "Go to your mother. She is your mother."

I suppose I had become fearful of her—in young children it happens.

One thing I had forgotten, or lost, when I returned was my Jamaican accent. By then I had a full-on New York brogue.

We lived in an apartment behind six different locks in the Bronx near the southern end of Crotona Park. I think a lot of Jamaicans lived in that building. The Bronx wasn't terrible then, but by the time I came, it wasn't all that great, either. It certainly wasn't the neighborhood that, say, former general Colin Powell, who grew up partly in the Bronx, remembers. His parents were Jamaican immigrants. I can remember the shrill of the train as it wound around the bend on the street outside. It was 1971. The times were dangerous. We had one of those rods in the floor that braced against the door lock so that even if somehow people got past the other locks, they couldn't push the door open.

I did get to play outside, but it was nothing like Jamaica. There was "going to the park." We had no such sayings in Jamaica. What did that mean? Well, it was my only outside play time, and it was scheduled. The park was within walking distance. It was a beautiful park, but I didn't ever go alone. The other outside time we got was hanging out on the fire escape. This was nice in warm weather. Yes, I can remember plenty of hot weather in New York, but mostly from my later years there in high school.

* * *

The first American school I went to was to PS 61, which was near Crotona Park on the park's east side. That's how they named the schools
in New York. "PS" stands for "public school." I had come to America
perhaps too prepared for school. Back in Jamaica, I had already started
primary school, as we called it. I had gone to Mrs. Barnes's School.
Boy, Mrs. Barnes *beat* us all the time! It was acceptable at the time
to whack with ruler and cane. She didn't have anything particular
against me. She beat my cousins, too. She just beat everybody! At
the time, we had slate tablets, we wrote with slate instruments. We
learned our ABCs and 123s. I think I was three or four years old when
I started school. That's not unusual in Jamaica, either. We were raised
on the British education system. One thing the British did right was
to bring education to the colonies.

At PS 61, I was coming home every week with some kind of award.
We began by spelling words like "this," "that," "where," "when."

I was happy living with my father, sister, and Annette, but school
had proved to be neither engaging nor much of a challenge. I was list-
less when I was there, and in much better spirits when I was home. I
was simply not learning enough in America.

Finally, my grandmother Valda came up. She could tell immediately that I was not thriving. Those were her words: "not thriving." She
consulted with my father and they made the decision that it was better
for me to come back to Jamaica, at least for a few years.

I was nine when I returned to Jamaica.

It's probably not a surprise to many that the elementary schools
were not so great in the Bronx. But to Jamaicans at the time, America
was what they saw in movies and television. There weren't a lot of films
that depicted inner-city schools of the early 1970s, I guess.

So I boarded yet another Pan Am jetliner and headed back to my
grandmother's house.

* * *

I attended Greenwich Primary School. We called elementary school "primary school," after the Brits. When my husband first visited Jamaica he commented on all the smaller children walking together to school, holding hands, all strolling in their crisp uniforms, brother and sister, siblings, cousins, holding hands walking each other to school.

Anyway, as a child we walked to a Kingston bus stop, took it to a stop near the school, and walked the rest of the way. I remember that bus route. Along the way, we passed the Chinese cemetery. The entrance had Chinese characters, and the tomb sites had pictures of the deceased on them. Then of course there was also the Jewish cemetery.

As a kid, we tried not to point at the graves as we went by. We had a saying that if you point at a cemetery, your finger would fall off. And if you did point, you would have to bite each finger to stop it from falling off.

My manner of dressing had made a subtle switch from English to American.

I wore Hush Puppies instead of Jumping Jacks. When I came to New York in the summers, I would buy some of my clothes for the year. But most people in Jamaica depended on their American relatives to send items they wanted or needed.

You might make an outline of your foot and send it up with someone visiting. When they returned, you got your shoes. Yes, we could have bought our shoes in Jamaica. But these were generally English imports, and we didn't want English shoes anymore. We wanted American sneakers.

With so many immigrants overseas, a custom arose among Jamaicans to send home barrels to Jamaica. It was a big, big deal there. People were ecstatic when the latest barrel came in. In America or Canada, the relative buys a blue plastic barrel or, in former times, a cardboard barrel. The barrel is about three or four feet tall and three feet wide. You then begin packing your barrel with items. You might do this over a three- or four-month period.

You pack it with rice. We love getting foodstuff. Jamaicans may be the original preppers. Maybe you throw in an iron, curtains, linens, shoes—whatever you can fit in a barrel that you think someone might need. Can openers, utensils, lotions, cosmetics, even perhaps a television if you can keep it from bouncing around and breaking. When you're done and all is ready, you twist on those locking tops. Then you ship it to Jamaica.

For decades, goods were much cheaper to buy in America and ship in a barrel than to buy in Jamaica, if they were even available. So much on the island is imported and costs more.

A few years ago, the Jamaican government got wise to the revenue they were losing. I'm also sure the shop owners were complaining. Now the government makes sure that to clear a barrel the taxes you pay are high. We're not shipping barrels as much anymore. But we did that for years and years. I remember it well. When the barrel arrived, it was Christmas! Often it *was* Christmas. But anytime a barrel arrived was cause for celebration.

"What's in the barrel? What's in the barrel?"

Now back in America, you had to be careful. If you tell too many people, "I'm packing a barrel," you may be in for trouble. You buy items for your family and pack them carefully. Fabric to make uniforms, put it in there. Books, school supplies, pack it carefully.

Then you start to get calls. People say, "I hear you are packing a barrel. Do you have room for this? I can send it with you!" If you're not careful, you have everybody else's items in the barrel, and nobody is paying you to ship it!

No, you had to keep it quiet. Tell only close family. Let the others pack their own barrel! It's the same with a suitcase. If people know you're going down to Jamaica it's, "Oh, can you take something for me?"

Pretty soon you don't have any room for your own stuff! Plus, you've gone over fifty pounds. Time to pay extra for overweight luggage. As a matter of fact, flight attendants know a plane going to Jamaica will be laden with heavy bags. They start distributing the carry-ons all over the plane in advance, otherwise, they have to waste time redoing it later. We stuff our bags to the gills, all right. And if it's bursting, we don't care. We put some rope or tape around it to hold it together.

You simply can't go empty-handed to Jamaica. It's not done. Everybody's waiting for something.

There were empty barrels in use throughout my grandmother's yard. We had a saying: Every mickle makes a muckle. Everything can serve more than one purpose. People use barrels to store all kinds of things. The blue ones were great for rainwater. They could withstand the elements.

* * *

Every year when I came up for summer vacation in New York, I felt like I was freezing. Can you imagine? Summer in New York was cold to me. I'd wear sweaters and coats, sometimes. People stared at me.

But not to me. I'd go out and sit in the sun. I had an uncle who used air-conditioning constantly, and I *hated* visiting. Freezing!

You come up in the summer, you have to go visit everybody. No exceptions. That's how it's done. Everybody wants to see how much you've grown. What's sprouting now.

"Lawd, shi getting big!"

Everybody wants to know how you're doing in school. You have to do well because people want to brag.

Visits were family reunion time for those in America. Time for a celebration. You had to spend the night with this sister, this cousin, this aunt, this in-law, otherwise people got upset.

I was on the tail end of the cousins migrating up. My uncle Ledley, my grandfather's brother, had a beautiful two-story brownstone in Brooklyn. My grandmother would frequently stay there when she came to visit. I was fascinated when I heard my grandmother and Ledley's wife speak. They were both "Mrs. Earle." They'd both married Earle brothers. Uncle Ledley's daughter Nadine was a classical concert pianist. My grandmother was like glue, very social; she had to visit everyone.

I felt like a nomad when it was my turn to come up as a child. Then finally all the family whirl would die down and I could stay with my father for a while.

* * *

When I came back to Jamaica at nine, I had a problem. I had fallen behind the level I would otherwise have been in Jamaican schools. The person who came to my rescue was my aunt Babs's husband, Aubrey. My aunt Violet (aka Aunt Babs) had returned from England a nurse. She'd been married one month when her first husband, Trevor, died in a terrible car accident. She later married Aubrey. Aubrey was educated at Harvard as an agronomist. He had been recruited in Jamaica by Harvard, and offered a scholarship. He took it, attended Harvard, then returned to Jamaica where he went to work for the Ministry of Agriculture.

Uncle Aubrey and I worked together to get me up to an appropriate educational level. In fact, he helped me so much that I moved a level ahead when I started back to school in Jamaica. He would get out the clock and teach me how to tell the time. He made multiplication tables and quizzed me on them over and over. In fact, Uncle Aubrey continued tutoring me on and off for several years. We were doing algebra by the fifth or sixth grade, or at least some form of distribution-type multiplication.

When I first returned to Jamaica, I was put into a private Catholic prep school. My father decided after half a year that he was not paying private-school tuition anymore. He said the public school had been good enough for him, and it should be good enough for me. He was right. I ended up at Greenwich Primary School.

Public schools were on par with private schools in Kingston. The requirements were similar and nobody advanced without learning. All was based on the British system.

Furthermore, there was corporal punishment. If you didn't learn, they were going to beat learning into you, I suppose. Of course, corporal punishment is not done any longer.

The expectation across the social and economic classes was that children are supposed to learn. It was the familiar refrain: You had to have a good education. You must try to make something of yourself.

Most Jamaican parents moved heaven and earth to get their kids into a good school. In a nation with fewer economic opportunities, this was one more or less guaranteed ticket to a comfortable life. At the end of primary school, the children of the entire nation took the Common Entrance Exam (the CEE). You needed to pass this, or your parents would have to pay for you to go to high school. Not everyone passed, so there were many mothers and fathers who worked multiple jobs to pay the school fee for their children at a decent high school. If you went to a good high school—and all were rigorously rated in a nationwide system—your future was invariably going to be brighter. Those parents knew it.

You could, starting at ten years old, take the CEE, which pits you against every child wanting to get into high school. There was no middle school when I was growing up. High school in Jamaica begins in the seventh grade.

The test was much like the PSAT, but gauged for ten- to thirteen-year-old kids. If you scored at a certain level, then at ten you could move into high school. If you'd aged out of the test at thirteen, then you could take a different test and perhaps get into a technical school, which was still likely a good school.

I ended up taking the test twice. When I took the test the first time, I was still catching up. The next year I took it and did well.

After the test, those who passed entered into a national selection process. This was not such an impossible project as it might be in the United States. Jamaica is not a huge place, remember. The current population is around two million people, which is around the present-day population of Idaho, Nebraska, or New Mexico. Furthermore, the vast majority of the Jamaican population lived in the Kingston area.

Families named three high schools that they wanted their child to attend. None of the schools had to be nearby. Then the schools made their selections from this pool of applicants based on their scores. So you were vying for a slot with all the Jamaican children who also picked one of your schools. The high schools themselves were rated. There were A high schools, Bs, and Cs. Parents and students knew these ratings going in.

When the selection process was done, the results were announced in the Kingston newspapers. Everyone would buy the paper and go through the huge lists of kids matched up with schools until they found their student. Then, with held breath, they would scan their eyes over to see which school it was to be. The process almost sounds like being accepted into college, doesn't it?

My three choices had been girl's schools. The school that chose me was listed as Camperdown High School. It was a great school, but it had not been on my list! It was all the way on the other side of Kingston from us.

The adults, including Aubrey, my mother, and my grandmother, got to work. They visited education and school offices. I don't know how they did it exactly, but I soon found myself accepted at another school that had also not been on my list. This was a coed high school called Ardenne.

* * *

For the next two years, I attended Ardenne High School. Most high schools in Jamaica were started by religious organizations. Ardenne had been founded by American Church of God missionaries George and Nellie Olson in 1927, and it became known for excellent academics.

In Jamaica at the time, all grade levels wore uniforms. These were not issued by the schools, and it was not a matter of going to Walmart or Target to pick up shirts and khakis. The schools issued their requirement. You then had to buy the material and find a seamstress to make the uniforms. The schools did not issue books to you. As in college in the United States, you had to buy them. During all this, we discovered that there had been a mistake. Instead of Camperdown, I had been admitted to a Catholic school called Holy Childhood High School. But the die was cast by then. I was going to Ardenne.

Your uniform became a source of pride, because right away you could tell which high school a person attended. Believe me, people knew if that school was an A school, a B school, or a C school.

We didn't have the word "nerd" in Jamaica. You were looked up to for being smart. Without an education, you were going nowhere.

We didn't use the term "grades." Just like in the British system, there were "forms." I started in first form, equivalent to seventh grade in the United States; second form was the eighth grade. I got to the second form, and then I left Jamaican school once again for America.

I would like to put in a word for the Jamaican education system of my time. The circumstances and challenges were far different in America, but there is a lot to be said for the Jamaican system. Jamaica was already a nation that had entered failure mode with the ascendancy of the left-wing demagogue Michael Manley to prime minister in 1972. The nation was on the way to leaving the people impoverished, keeping crime and safety a continuing problem, and letting an infrastructure crumble to pieces. But during my time there the education system performed admirably. The reason for this was the *parents*.

Of course Jamaican parents are no different from parents everywhere in one sense: They want the best for their children. They want their children to have a chance to do better than they did. Students knew it as well. If you have a family business that will pass to you, you can't be a dunce. You can't lose what the family has started. If you're rich you want your child to do well, and if you're poor you want your child to do well. Education is the way to achieve this.

People throughout history have felt the same, even when they were slaves. History and dozens of slave narratives have shown that if you were a slave, you wanted three things: Number one, you wanted your freedom. Number two, you wanted to be reunited with your family. But number three was, you wanted an education for yourself and your children. Slaves understood that education was the road out of poverty and powerlessness. The masters knew, too. That was why reading and writing were stifled in the old American South. A literate slave could write his own ticket to freedom.

In a Jamaican high school of my day, when the teacher came in, you stood. You did not sit down until instructed, no matter how old you were. Your school leaders came from the upper forms (grades). The Head Boy and Head Girl came from sixth form. Prefects came from fifth and sixth forms. Lower sixth form and upper sixth form equates to the senior year and first year of college. Leadership uniforms were different. Each lower form class had an upper form prefect assigned to it. These prefects were in charge of the children of their form, and particularly policed their behavior. The prefects would line you up each day to check your uniform. They would tell you, "Take that off" or "Put that on." They'd make sure we all had ties up, buttons buttoned. This extended to personal grooming, too. It wasn't unusual to hear, "Go comb your hair."

Sound familiar? Yes, it's almost like the military. I guess that's why I was not so shocked at similar treatment in the Marine Corps.

"Why is your uniform not ironed?"

"Where is your emblem?"

"Where is your school pin?"

"Tie that tie properly!"

"You get a demerit!"

"You get detention!"

These were our student leaders. Yes, for some, leadership got to their heads. And kids naturally rebel at times, giving them plenty of fodder for handing out demerits. It was easy to get resentful. "These kids are acting like they're my mom and dad, and I already have parents!" But the bullies were by far the exception. Prefects were often the most mature and balanced sixth formers. It's not as if they were akin to a class president and voted in. No, they were appointed. They were the chosen ones. We respected them because we knew the adults trusted them. They were smart, too, and we wanted to be like them. We valued what they'd learned and accomplished. They were our advocates with the teachers as well as our disciplinarians.

And the truth is, everybody wanted to be a prefect when they got older. One reason was that then *you* got to tell everybody what to do! But the main reason was that it was a position of respect and responsibility.

The entirety of sixth form wore different uniforms as well. The whole class was looked up to as leaders.

Our Ardenne uniform was a full-length tunic. But when you got to the sixth form, as a female, you would wear a blue skirt, a white top, and a tie. Generally, no matter your high school, the prefects wore something white. They would wear a white top of some kind, or a white shirt. When you were at a bus stop you could tell who the sixth form kids were. You knew who the prefects and other leaders were just by looking at the uniforms. They got a certain amount of deference even outside of school.

During those years, I would come back every year to America to my dad's, mostly in the summers, sometimes during holidays. It was understood that I was going to end up in America when all was said and done. Since high school in America started in the ninth grade, the decision was made—and this time I was a part of it—that I would move back to New York and finish high school there.

Chapter Four

JAMAICA, FAITH, AND JESUS

Before I turn my attention entirely to America, I want to linger in the Jamaica of my youth a bit longer. In so many ways, that island childhood with its steady connection to my father via Pan Am flights provided the central support beams of my character. It is what I have built on since, and that Jamaican girl full of wonder, determination, mangos, and rice and peas underlies everything I am and whatever I do.

First of all, the political system of Jamaica, full of failed socialist and Marxist schemes, has left the nation in a third world status for decades. While small nations such as the Asian tigers of Thailand and Taiwan were powering up, adapting capitalism to their cultures, and rising from poverty, Jamaica, with its politics firmly turned to the left, managed to miss every opportunity for growth, the equal protection of rights, and the transition to a law-based society. It didn't start out badly, but it surely ended up in terrible condition for far too long.

I am glad that America provided opportunities for us. Indeed, many immigrants return to the country of their birth to plant the seeds of freedom they found in the United States.

Socialism was disastrous for Jamaica.[1] When the extreme left-winger Michael Manley won an election and came to power in 1972, one of his stated goals was to bring the races together and uplift the Black man. This was a movement in the former colonies of Africa at the time. You can read about its dismal failure in books such as V. S. Naipaul's *A Bend in the River*. Socialism is supposed to be share and share alike, except it doesn't ever work like that. The tendency of man is to be selfish. Socialism doesn't work wherever it's been tried. I don't care if people talk about the Swedish model, either. Even the Scandinavian countries have repudiated it for the most part these days, and are at heart capitalist systems.

I remember as a child the big word-change operation Manley tried to establish. Instead of a "maid," the person would now be called a "helper," for instance. But the maid was still doing the same job, of course! Sound familiar?

Socialism destroys productivity. A man with two donkeys can do not just two times, but *many* times the work of a man with only one. How? Humans are clever. They know how to use advantages to multiply force. It might not be two donkeys. It might be access to a water-wheel's power, a couple of trucks, whatever. The government comes along and says, "Why do you have two donkeys? That's not fair!" So they take one donkey from you and give it to somebody else. What is lost is not just the strength of that one donkey to the man. What is lost is that man's ability to produce five or ten times what he had accomplished with two donkeys.

Kingston real estate value was destroyed as well as properties throughout the island. Government offices stopped paying rent in privately held property where they'd paid rent before. Manley called Jamaica a banana republic and went to war against the multinational corporations with bases in the country. Then Manley came in and destroyed everything.

Of course people began to complain. The answer from Manley was, "There's a plane that leaves every day at three p.m. for Miami. If you don't like my economic policies, you can get on it."

That was exactly what a lot of people did—so many, in fact, that he passed currency conversion limits to keep them from taking their money along with them.

It was economic madness.

When my father came to America in 1963, he would send money back home for me and my mom. At the time, before socialism, the Jamaican dollar was worth more than the American dollar, so she would convert it and put it in savings. That ended under Manley's regime.

Manley did do a few good things. He put decent adult literacy programs in place, as well. Eventually, it all came home to roost. The insane interest on government bonds came due and there was no money to pay them. The foreign debt was enormous. The International Monetary Fund (IMF) had blundered in, and he borrowed even more money from them. IMF came to be known as "Is Manley Fault."

Michael Manley's policies destroyed Jamaica. He brought Castroism and Cubans over and put them in positions of influence. He took Russian money, started filling schools with Marxist teachers, and instigated a command economy.

It got to the point where the people tired of Manley. As I've heard reported, Jamaica badly needed foreign exchange (U.S. dollars), so illegal marijuana exports brought it in. You had garrison neighborhoods ruled by gunmen. Rastafarians had generally stayed out of politics before this. They were for peace and love. No more. The changing situation even drove Bob Marley out of Jamaica. He was almost killed because of local gangster politics.

Michael Manley was a class-driven politician. He had married a Black woman, but he'd gone through multiple wives. Yet, he was like a Pied Piper to the populace. Still, he didn't fool anyone who was paying attention. There was a brain drain, as the best and brightest fled Jamaica and took their talents elsewhere. Many multinational companies eventually shut down and left. Manley had a habit of nationalizing anything profitable, and they found their investments were no longer their own.

The poor stayed because they had to, but most of the rich left. After a while there was no longer much of a middle class. The professionals left. There was no reliable tax base, so there was no money for infrastructure. Everything began a slow process of collapse. Finally the people voted him out of office in 1980. But then they voted him back in again in 1989–1992![2]

In the end, he apologized.

"Defeat concentrates the mind considerably and besides, it gives you time to rest," Manley said at the time.[3]

He knew he'd destroyed Jamaica. But it was too late. Many people were long gone by then.

Because the government kept printing money to fund this and that, inflation got totally out of control. The shelves became bare all the time. You were restricted in the number of items you could buy at a time. The regime put in place many crazy price control gimmicks, as well. There was this practice where food items were "married" at the store. You weren't allowed to buy chicken unless you also bought something else with it, usually something you didn't need or want to spend the money on. It was an insane way to try to reduce demand. There were multiple limits on item amounts.

We would stand outside a store, and my grandmother would give the children money and say, "You don't know me." Each of us was given a list that divided up the family needs. We'd buy what the family required, not what the government dictated. Each of us would go through the line separately, and then meet up outside.

If you want to talk about bringing socialism to the United States, go peddle that elsewhere. Don't tell me. I saw what it did. It doesn't work.

* * *

You could say practically everybody feels like they know God in Jamaica. It's a very religious country. Christianity is the biggest influence. The Church of England, the Anglican Church, was for years the official church, and Anglicans founded many schools and institutions. There is also Catholicism. These versions of Christianity are sometimes mixed with several African religions, as well. There is a distinct Jewish tradition and heritage on the island from far back in history. There are, of course, Muslims and Hindus among the East Indian and Arab families. The Chinese brought with them their religions and beliefs. Then there also are Rastafarians, who follow Haile Selassie, the former emperor of Ethiopia!

There were certain African customs that I ran into occasionally. These were animistic religions, so they were looked down upon. Jamaica is by and large mostly Christian. There was something we called the Junkanoo. It's a mixture of African animism and other religions.

There is also a group of people called Maroons who held themselves apart. They were people who had escaped slaves in their ancestry. They have defined sovereign territory in Jamaica, much as Native Americans do in the United States. In the historic past they lived deep in the middle of the mountain forests. One group was led by a female warrior, "Nanny," whose warriors occasionally descended to burn plantations and kill the White people there. After trying to exterminate them and failing, the British decided to leave them alone. They signed a treaty to end hostilities.

So there is some racial mix. It's a melting pot of many people. It's an island. You have to get along. In Jamaica, people fought it out and eventually melded.

We are Christians. My grandmother was Catholic, but it was an evangelical form of Catholicism. We would often see her kneel down by her bedside in the mornings. She would take the end of the sheet and put it over her entire body. We understood as grandchildren that you shouldn't bother Mommy when she was praying to God.

We were often in Protestant churches. Later in life, Mommy attended a Catholic church; however, most of the time, we attended a Protestant church called Olivet. Although we were always in church, for some reason I had not heard the Gospel, never experienced it in my heart, that is. I'm sure we talked about Jesus in Sunday school, but I don't remember us discussing His great purpose on Earth.

My grandmother put her Christian faith into action. We had it a little better than most, so she bought clothes and shoes for other children who were poorer.

My paternal grandmother once brought a homeless man into our house. He was dirty and as high on marijuana as one can be, eyes shot through with red. As a small child, I could not see the good she was doing. I could only think about the smell. But not only did Mommy bring this man home, she set him up for a meaningful life.

She got him in adult literacy class, and found a job for him while he was going to the class. He was brought back into a real life, a good life. I've talked with him in the years since, and this intervention held. It changed his life.

That is just one example of the many things I saw and experienced with my grandmother. She was inspirational. So it's no wonder that I became, for instance, the director of a homeless shelter. It's how I know that education can lift a person out of poverty. I saw it happen. I know it will work. If you have the determination, there are people who will help. There are far more programs in the United States than there are in Jamaica. This man made a success of himself. He wasn't the only one my grandmother helped, either.

My grandfather Gilbert was a quiet influence on me, as well. I remember him urging my older cousins to get a trade. He told them that a college degree was wonderful, but the skill acquired in a trade can never be taken from you. You can find a way to make a living with your hands no matter what. He himself was a mechanic. His trade had seen him through the Depression. People always need a mechanic. They always need a carpenter. Or a welder. An electrician. That's one of the reasons why, when I joined the Marine Corps, I became an electrician. I remembered that advice from my grandfather.

* * *

It wasn't until I was twelve years old that I heard a visiting Sunday School teacher in one of our breakout classes talk about this man and how he died on the cross for us. This particular Sunday school was not at Olivet, our normal church. It was a little church on the hill near Aunt Babs. I had moved over to live with my aunt Babs and her husband. I became a child they could help to raise. I would also move back and forth to and from my mom and grandmother.

I wondered when I heard this message from the teacher. Why would someone die for another he did not know? Why would he die for me? What kind of a love could be so great that Jesus would die for someone else? The thought fascinated me. So when the class was over and it was time to go back inside, I asked the teacher if he could tell me more about this man Jesus. And when I heard, I decided right then that I would accept Him as my Savior, as the substitute for my sins. He was willing to take all of my sins, all of my evil thoughts, disobedience, defiance, envy, hatred, mean acts, *everything* on Himself because of His great love for me. I would be forgiven. And not only forgiven once, but for all time.

I thought, how can I not love someone who loves me enough to die for me?

I remember the very moment that I accepted Him. I felt like I was walking on cloud nine. I felt like I was not touching the ground. It was an amazing experience for a twelve-year-old.

People might say to me that you can't really know God when you're so young. I would reply to them that they have no clue what a true conversion experience feels like. I *know* that happened to me then. I believed that there was a God when I was twelve years old, and that He cared for me.

At the time, I never really told anyone else. There seemed no way to talk about it. So I went on living.

And I began to slide away. I knew the right things to do, but did not do them.

I did return to the Lord's fold eventually—more on that later. We've tried to raise our girls as I wish I had been raised. Each of my children had her own Bible. Until they left for college, we had family devotions every day. We read from the Bible, and we discussed it. Terry and I made sure that they understood what they believed and why they believed it. If they had doubts and questions, we would talk things through, we would discuss them. They had to decide for themselves whether they believed this man Jesus was worthy or not. I had none of that when I was their age. When you know differently, you do differently.

People often call me bold. Some use it as a term of admiration. Whatever the case, I certainly get a lot of my boldness from being a Marine. But I would say that I get more of my boldness from God. He is the ultimate, is He not? We see in Revelation 3:8, "See, I have placed before you an open door that no one can shut. I know that you have little strength, yet you have kept my word and have not denied my name."[4] If He opens the door for you, who can shut it?[5]

Nothing happens that He doesn't know will happen. He holds the future in His hand. He orchestrates everything. There is no one greater, and the result is that I try always to fear not. He is with me. He was with me in Jamaica. He would be with me in America as I was about to make the biggest change of my young life.

Chapter Five

AMERICAN TEEN

When I was fifteen, I decided I wanted to pursue my dreams in America. Although I hadn't loved the educational system so far, even at a young age I had seen the promise of America. I'd seen my father and my relatives working hard and making something of themselves. You could be prosperous and free in America on an entirely different level than was possible in Jamaica.

My father traveled to Jamaica to finally say he wished me to come to America. He talked to my mom and asked me about what I wanted to do. My mother and I talked. We understood this was for good. It was going to be a major upheaval. I made the decision; my mom made the decision. America had the opportunities.

"Dad," I said, "we decided. I'd like to stay in America for good."

By this time my father had bought a home. It was a triplex where he was both homeowner and landlord. My grandmother had come up one year and said to him, "It's time for you to own. All this apartment living is not good." She proceeded to go out and track down the property where he now lived.

He'd moved around a lot after I'd originally come, especially after he and Annette had gotten a divorce. The area he'd settled in was a better part of the Bronx at the time.

Adlai E. Stevenson High School was several blocks away from

where we lived. I took the city bus to school. In New York City, we used public transport and not school buses.

High school in Kingston and at Stevenson High School in the Bronx was like being on two different planets. Back in Jamaica, the kids showed a lot more respect for their teachers. When a teacher came into the room, you stood up, politely said in unison with your classmates, "Good morning, Mr. or Mrs. So-and-So," and you did not sit until you were told.

Stevenson was a culture shock. The few outliers were in the honors classes. I couldn't wrap my head around it. Respect for the teachers was not what it should have been. It seemed everyone was constantly talking.

Like I said, there were no "nerds" back in Jamaica. We were all competitive bookworms. We had such high expectations for ourselves, without even knowing it. The alternative to hard work was practically unknown. Nobody wanted to suffer the consequences of going home and showing our parents bad grades. We couldn't even fathom the thought.

My dad tried to get me into the honors classes by showing off my transcripts. In Jamaica, high school begins in seventh grade, and I was about to go into ninth grade. I had already taken (and aced!) biology, chemistry, and physics. But the bureaucrats didn't believe us. They said, "No. What you took was 'general science.'" So they wouldn't bend and they put me in the regular ninth-grade science classes. Needless to say, I quickly started soaring through them, and then I was moved into the honors classes.

Looking back, the schools in Jamaica provided not only a top-notch education but also excellent character formation, as do many other Commonwealth countries that operate under the British system. We need to be more careful with how we talk about "third world countries"!

As I noted before, my classmates at Stevenson were also different. There was a group of girls who were the bullies.

We had a chemistry teacher who didn't have control of the class. She wasn't used to disruptive kids.

So the classroom was in complete disarray, and I was sitting in the front trying to listen. One day when Sharon (not her real name), the meanest of the mean girls, was yammering away, I lost it. I spun around in my chair and boomed, "Can you just stop talking!? I'm trying to learn! If you don't want to learn, that's fine. But I want to learn!"

Who told me to say that? I don't know, but I couldn't help myself. Sharon was unimpressed.

"I'm going to see *you* after school," she sneered.

The bell rang. Class was dismissed for the day. Word had gotten around school because, well, somehow word just gets around school. It seemed like all of Stevenson was there in the field that afternoon. Sharon had her whole crew lined up in a semicircle. I had my one friend, Hyacinth.

Although the odds weren't at all in my favor because Sharon was bigger, stronger, and meaner, she was going to have to fight me. And she was going to have to fight me good. Right when it seemed we were about to come to blows, a calm washed over me.

"We can fight, and you'll probably win," I yelled to Sharon across the way. She was grinning and nodding in agreement. I continued, "But we'll both get thrown out of school."

Now, I couldn't afford to get thrown out of school because my father would have killed me, probably literally. "I want to graduate and get out of here. I want to make something of myself," I continued, and then I asked, "What do you want? Do you want to stay here the rest of your life? Tell me!"

Her face changed. Something clicked in Sharon.

"You know what?" she replied. "You're right."

That was it. I think somehow she wanted someone to finally tell her that enough was enough. No child, however unruly, comes to school every day with the intention to learn *nothing*. Kids want to learn, but when they are frustrated time and again, they lose their way. They become part of the problem.

Sharon backed down. Not only that, but incredibly, we became friends afterward—and along with Sharon came her whole crew. My entire high school experience changed for the better.

Of course my very best friend remained Hyacinth, the girl who had my back. We are close to this day. Hyacinth also came from Jamaica, by the way. Today she owns her own business and has a PhD!

* * *

I spent those high school years doing the things a young woman in the Bronx might. I didn't really hang out with my friends. I spent a lot of time with my extended family, many of whom lived in New York or nearby. I had an American adolescence. Because I loved learning, many of my activities centered around school and the honors program at Stevenson.

My father never remarried after the divorce. Our relationship was always strong. We were like two peas in a pod during those years. I was the son he never had, in a sense. We'd watch the fights on television. We'd drink beer together. Alcohol drinking among the young is more relaxed in Jamaica, similar to Italian families drinking wine.

We *loved* watching Bugs Bunny cartoons together. We went together to house and yard get-togethers and neighborhood parties. He'd offer me a tiny glass of sherry when his buddies were over. So I'd sip a sherry with the men as they watched a game or sat around talking. This is not unusual in Jamaican families.

Dad was strict, though. He never used physical punishment, no spanking or anything, but discipline was key. He kept very close tabs on my grades, and generally knew where I was and who I was hanging out with.

He lives in Georgia now. He has a quiet life. He is still looking after my character. He doesn't want me to get a big head. When I was appointed to the Virginia State Board of Education, I called him to tell him about it.

I finished up and exclaimed, "Well, Dad, say something!"

"Yes, I heard," he replied. Then he changed the subject to something else he wanted to talk about.

I interrupted him after a while and said, "Wait a minute, do you understand what I'm telling you? The governor of Virginia just personally appointed me to an important board that oversees education! That's a big deal."

He said, "I heard you. It is a very big deal." Then he continued talking about whatever he'd been discussing.

Later on when I visited him down in Georgia, his friends told me about how proud he was and how he talked about me all the time.

* * *

I'm a huge *Star Trek* fan. I love all the various versions, but particularly the original series.

I liked the character of Uhura best of all, the communications officer on the starship USS *Enterprise*. In a way, that character was a role model, a Black woman who was performing a vital function on a grand, important mission—a *five-year mission* to go where no man had gone before, no less!

I later saw Nichelle Nichols, the actress who played Uhura, talking about an encounter she had with Dr. Martin Luther King Jr.

Nichols had been stung by being called the show's token Black character. She also considered herself a musical theater person. When she met Dr. King, she told him she was thinking about quitting *Star Trek*.

Dr. King said he and his family were huge *Star Trek* fans. He urged her not to quit. "Your role is not a *Black* role, and it's not a female role." He told her he approved of this vision of the future where Black people "will be seen as we should be seen every day, as intelligent, quality, beautiful people...who can go in space."[1, 2] He emphasized that she wasn't playing a ditzy maid or Innocent Andy. She was playing an intelligent woman, a vital part of the starship crew. Nichols decided to stay, and she became an inspiration to generations of Black women, and people in general, to explore the cosmos. She died not too long ago, and I believe a portion of her ashes are set to be launched into space for dispersal.[3]

Another favorite show of mine was *Julia*, with Diahann Carroll as a nurse named Julia Baker. She was the widowed mother of a boy, Corey. It was a sitcom, but with elements of drama. Julia was a competent, strong woman making her way in life. She reminded me of my aunt Babs. It's amazing, the detail with which I remember those shows! When we, as Black people, saw somebody Black on television, we would note it, we'd point it out, and be excited about it.

I graduated early with merit from Stevenson in January 1982, instead of the usual summer graduation. I was going to go to college in the fall. Truly, I can't remember what college it was, with all that happened directly after. SUNY? CUNY? Queens College? I do remember going to pick up my curriculum and buying my books. I was set to start in late August.

What do they say? Man plans and God laughs.

* * *

I flew to Jamaica in March for my eighteenth birthday. I wanted my grandmother to know I was succeeding, that I was going to excel, that all the effort she'd put into me was not for naught.

She said, "You're going to go to college, right?"

I answered, "Yes, of course I'm going to college."

My mom threw me a great party, many relatives and friends came, and we had fun. Later my grandmother said to me, "You're not going to see me alive again."

I replied, "But why are you saying this to me? There's nothing wrong with you."

She hadn't been ill. She was seventy-five, yes, but there was nothing wrong with her. She had diabetes, but she'd had that from the time I knew her, and she'd kept it under control. She took a pill for it daily.

It was July 1982. I got the call in New York from my cousin Paul. I was staying at my girlfriend Hyacinth's house. Hyacinth was the one who was with me back when the girls had threatened to beat me up in high school. I awakened from a dream. In the dream, I wore black and my grandmother was being lowered into the ground. I could see purple all around her, purple fabric, a purple glow. She was surrounded by flowers. Purple means mourning in Jamaica.

Hyacinth shook me awake from the dream. "Your cousin is on the phone," she said.

When I got the phone, Paul confirmed what I somehow already knew.

"Mommy's dead."

*   *   *

In Jamaican terms we would say that my grandmother had "come to tell me herself that she had died." Of course we have miracles in America. Look at George Washington's coat! Four bullets in it, yet he wasn't shot. The Revolution itself was miraculous.

There's a spiritual aspect to our lives. I understand that politicians are afraid to talk about it, but I absolutely believe that we're surrounded by a spiritual world. The things I have accomplished are part of a godly mission—and so are the things you have accomplished or are going to accomplish. I'm not ashamed to say it and to talk about it.

In Jamaica there is a ritual called Nine Nights. It's perhaps influenced by African customs. You prepare food every night for nine nights, and the whole community comes.

Everyone sorrows with you for nine days before the funeral. You have all kinds of foods. It's a celebration of the life of the deceased. It also gives the family things to do. People come by to sit and talk. They keep them company by playing dominoes, and so on.

Because the relatives are so spread out, sometimes the person isn't buried until three weeks later. People arrived daily from overseas. Everyone had to return from the various countries to which we'd spread. It was a testament to my grandmother's indomitable influence and love. All these people felt they *must* come back. Again, this is not unusual in Jamaican families.

At the church, I looked at her in the casket. People take pictures of those in the caskets; it's part of the culture. All I could do was gaze upon her that one last time.

I didn't go to the burial.

I left with my mother. I just couldn't do it. I couldn't witness that. While you watch, they lower the casket into a concrete vault and bury it. Then the masons mix cement right there and build the grave area. It takes a good hour or so of watching. And we're singing as we watch this activity. They level it off, corner it. They build a structure right in front of you.

I just couldn't deal with that for my beloved grandmother.

I was so affected because she loved me so greatly. She'd done so much for me. I thought of all the love that she had given me and I was overcome by one thought—what's the point? What was the point of life if you're just going to end up in a casket anyway?

As you can tell, my Christian faith was not what it should have been at the time. It had not been carefully nurtured. I was never discipled. Now I understand the hope that is there, even in death. When I speak of my grandmother I use the present tense. "Is," not "was."

To me she's more alive now than she ever was. I know I'm going to see her someday.

But my eighteen-year-old mind couldn't deal with her death. She was gone. What was there to live for now?

I truly felt like my life was over. My lines had been cut. I was adrift. Mommy was gone.

I was so distraught. I remained at my mother's for days.

At some point I said to her, "I'm just going to stay in Jamaica and die."

There was no reason to live. Mommy was gone. All the life she'd had, all the love she gave. Her influence in the community. The people she helped but could help no more.

After a while, my mother saw she had to snap me out of it.

She told me that if I were planning to stay in Jamaica and die, there were a few rules I'd have to obey around the house while I was dying.

She proceeded to lay them out.

"You must be home at a reasonable hour. You must find a job."

She laid out several chores I'd be expected to do.

Well, that didn't sit well with me at all. I was eighteen years old. An adult! Nobody could tell me what to do. She's trying to put me back under her thumb!

I began to come out of my stupor, but I was still not in the right frame of mind.

"Fine then, I'm going back to America," I told her.

Now, of course, I see exactly what Mom was doing. She knew what it would take for me to find the will to live. That was why she said what she said.

Later, I think it may have been that same day, I was sitting on her couch fuming—but mostly feeling utterly lost. I listlessly looked around for something to distract me.

My mother happened to have a *Jet* magazine on her coffee table. I opened it up randomly. It fell open to a full-page advertisement for the U.S. Marine Corps.

There was a picture of a Marine. Wow, he looked so stoic and tough. Below the photo was that great advertising motto: "The Few. The Proud. The Marines."

I thought to myself: Yes, that's what I need. Discipline. The Marine Corps will give that to me. They will give me a reason to live.

So I flew back to America and joined the Marine Corps.

Boy, did they give me reasons to live. And the discipline I needed.

The Marines, it turned out, saved my life and gave me a future.

Chapter Six

BOOT CAMP

The saying goes, "And God created the drill instructor, and then there was Hell."

I flew back to the Bronx.

My next clear memory is of arriving upstate at the Armed Forces Examining and Entrance Station, the AFEE station, as I would learn to call it.

When I arrived, I found there were four lines. People were lined up under the branch of service for which they had been recruited. The Army and Air Force lines seem to stretch down to the water, through the woods, and over the plains. The Navy line was a bit shorter.

But in the Marine Corps line? There were only four of us. I was the only woman.

I thought, Oh hell, what did I get myself into?

* * *

At that time (is it still so?), if you were on the East Coast, then you went to Parris Island, South Carolina, for Marine boot camp. Otherwise you went to Marine Corps Recruit Depot San Diego. We called them Hollywood Marines. They didn't get the sand fleas. There's long been that rivalry in the Corps, the Parris Island Marines versus the Hollywood Marines. We're still all Marines.

So we got on a plane and then we flew down to, I believe, either somewhere in South Carolina or Savannah. We then boarded a bus in the dead of night bound for Parris Island. That bus drove through a portion of the country I'd never seen before: the rural South.

I saw shanties. I saw houses that were falling over, but people still lived in them. I thought if I told anyone in Jamaica that people were living like this in America they would call me a liar. Jamaicans would never believe such types of houses existed in America.

What I was seeing was definitely not the America we heard about. It wasn't the one I'd experienced while growing up in the Bronx. I'd grown up in New York America. There were beautiful streets, there were sturdy buildings, skyscrapers of metal and glass.

No skyscrapers around here. I was driving through the coastal Deep South. And they were speaking with an accent I didn't understand. I was from New York! I couldn't figure out half of what the drill instructors said at first.

My drill instructors were all female in 1982. Now it's more integrated with men and women drill instructors, I believe, but generally the male drill instructors train the men, and the women train the women. Occasionally you would have a class with a male instructor.

But the screaming, the psychological games? Oh, yes, I got all that. I don't think we slept for the first three days. But, of course, that was to break you down. They're trying to make you part of the team. Sleep deprivation is a useful tool. Every time they saw you falling asleep, they were in your face, "Wake up! Wake up!"

Your whole system is jolted. There's a reason they bring you into boot camp at night. They bring you in when you are already tired and disoriented.

Half of the time at first they thought I was being rebellious, when in actuality what they'd just shouted at me sounded like gibberish. My instructors had Southern drawls. Furthermore, they were dragging out everything they said, putting even more of an accent on it.

They were breaking us down so that they could rebuild us into

Marines. And by the way, we were not called "Marine" until we graduated boot camp. You had to earn the title. You were "Recruit," and
other names.

I'm not saying that the other armed forces aren't tough, but Marines
are an extreme example of the American warrior. We're just different
that way.

My best friend, Hyacinth, had gone into the Army. I remember
when I came home from boot camp, I saw pictures Hyacinth had
taken at her Army basic training. She was posing comfortably on the
rack—what we called the bed—and doing all kinds of fun things in
her free time. Let me tell you, I didn't have that on Parris Island.

We didn't know which way was up. They don't treat the women
any differently, mentally or psychologically. Bullets don't know male
from female. Bullets don't care. We had to know how to shoot our
M16A rifles. I learned how to pull that thing apart in under two minutes, all the way down to the cotter pin.

A Marine, male or female, has to be able to shoot properly. He has
to be able to clean the weapon properly. Everyone is a rifleman. All
Marines must be prepared to protect and defend. This is not Sunday
school. This is life and death. This is war.

You should not become a Marine or join any military service merely
to get money for college. Yes, you will get that. Yes, there are benefits.
But when a drill instructor puts an automatic rifle in your hands and
tells you that this is your best friend, you realize the world is not as
you knew it.

I loved the discipline of it. It was exactly what I needed at that time
in my life. I loved the camaraderie and the take-no-prisoners attitude.

In many ways, it felt like home. I'd grown up in a household of
expectations. We didn't make any excuse; we didn't cry about being
in a third world country. No, we were expected to make something of
ourselves no matter where we started.

I also loved the feeling of belonging.

"We are the Marines. We are few. Not everybody can get in."

Another Marine Corps saying goes, "When you are the finest, it's hard to be humble."

*   *   *

The Marines call initial training "boot camp." We don't have drill sergeants; we have drill instructors. We lived in what was called the squad bay. The barracks is the whole building. The squad bay is the living area for your platoon. It's an open squad bay at boot camp.

There were seventy women in my platoon. You are called the Women Marines, the WMs—

That is, *after* you get out of boot camp. In boot camp, you are a mere recruit.

By the time I came on board, they had gotten rid of the blue uniforms WMs had previously worn. Now we were one Marine Corps, and everyone wore the olive drab and the light khaki. The women were not to be singled out. You're a Marine; you will dress like a Marine.

I was screamed at from left to right. I had three drill instructors screaming at me constantly from the east, west, north, and south. Or was it four? At first I had no idea what to do. I was always confused. That was by design.

We learned to stand at attention. Oh boy, that's a whole different matter at Parris Island. There are these evil creatures known as sand fleas.

Parris Island sand fleas are not like any pest you've ever encountered. They are insects,[1] not crustaceans, and they are so mean that they prey on mosquitoes! They are very tiny, about a hundredth of an inch long, and they look like a speck of dirt if you see them at all, which you usually don't.

But you feel them. Oh yes, you do.

They bite like the dickens. They come in swarms. They are like the Terminator. They do not feel pity. They do not feel remorse. And they absolutely will not stop biting you.

When we stood at attention, we were not supposed to do anything. We were supposed to let them bite us. You're at attention, and at attention you don't move, regardless. But the sand fleas never, ever let up.

You simply can't deal with it at some point. You start squirming to fend them off. But you can't, because there are so many of them, they're worse than gnats. Then the drill instructor screams at you, "You'd better not touch those sand fleas, recruit. Those are government issued!"

This may seem funny now, but at the time it was no laughing matter.

My hair was so much trouble to maintain in boot camp. Early on, one of my drill instructors said to me, "Private Earle, if you know like *I* know, and I *know* you know like *I* know, you will *cut your hair.*"

You don't have time to shampoo long hair in boot camp. That luxury doesn't exist. There were seventy of us women, and not many shower stalls in the barracks. We only get an hour to shower. So there were, of necessity, five of us in a shower at a time.

Sometimes my childhood in Jamaica felt like the Corps. One of my chores was to dust. When I told my grandmother or mother that I was done dusting, I had to prove it.

"Come here and write your name on this table," she'd say.

And if she couldn't see my name, then I'd done the job.

If not, I had to dust again. And on top of that I would get something else to do because I hadn't done a good job in the first place. So when the Marine Corps would give me the "white glove test," I would think, "oh, I know all about this."

Of course it was on a whole different level. Drill instructors are not speaking softly. They are screaming at you, and it's very public.

It's all about accountability. Carrying your own weight.

My drill instructors purposely came up with things to make us laugh so they could discipline us even more.

Nobody laughs. Heavens, if you laugh, that drill instructor will make a mockery of *you.*

There's the famous Marine recruit long stare. You don't look at anyone when you are a recruit. You look *through* them. You try to look past them.

It was bright lights. Deafening sounds. Hurry up and do this and that. Stress levels were high. Your life is not your own. These strangers have so much power over you that you can't even blink unless they told you. They told you when you could go to the bathroom.

"And by the way," they'd say, "I know what you're thinking and you'd better not think that, either!"

*   *   *

At boot camp, you want to please your drill instructors. They take the place of your family. They pull things out of you that you don't even realize you're capable of. A mom sends her son off to Marine Corps boot camp and he couldn't even boil water when he left. He comes back a whole different person. He comes back a responsible adult male who speaks with authority. He has what we called "bearing." He walks with authority!

And it's exactly the same with WMs. You stand straighter. You sit up. You say, "Yes sir. No ma'am." You're respectful.

Most of all, you feel as if you have purpose.

That's the enlisted experience. You'd have to ask my husband about the officer experience. Since they must lead, they have to be ready from day one when they graduate to do so.

During boot camp, my drill instructors kept trying to make me a leader among the enlisted. The truth was, I never wanted a leadership role at the time. I didn't want to be responsible.

Then one day, they just made me do it.

"Private Earle, you are the squad leader."

I couldn't say no.

I got punished for everything my squad did not do properly. Finally I gathered up the squad. Here I was, probably 110 pounds wet, and

I said to my squad, "If I have to do *one* more push-up for you, you're not going to like it. It's not going to be pretty! You'd better shape up!"

I must have scared them. We did shape up.

From my perspective, I was just trying to make it through boot camp. I was looking to forget myself, not find myself.

We had three drill instructors assigned to us. One was Italian. She was tinier than me, but man, she was a spitfire. The other one was perhaps of Irish descent. The gunny was White. They didn't care what color we were. They were going to make us Marines or we were going home. Marines are not Black, White, and so on. We are green.

Other instructors passed through in charge of various training. I'd shown one of them some brashness or disregard that she didn't like. She shouted, "Private Earle, with your New York attitude, you're not going to make it. You're *not. Going.* To *make. It.* You understand me?"

Until then I'd adopted my so-so attitude, trying to float through. If I make it, I make it, I'd decided. But once I heard that I thought, *Wait a minute!* I can't go home a failure. I *have* to graduate! I *must* graduate! I *will* become a Marine. They can't tell me what I can be and what I cannot be!

Those drill instructors were very crafty. This one had figured me out. If she'd said that to a different recruit, that recruit might have replied, "You bet; I'm out of here." They get to know us better than we know ourselves.

That was all I needed to hear. You don't tell me I'm going to fail. Nobody tells me I'm not going to make it. I dictate my life. You don't dictate my life.

One day toward the end, a drill instructor came into our squad bay and lined us up.

She said, "Recruits, you're going to graduate. And we're giving you back your lives."

That was when we realized just how much power these drill instructors had possessed over us.

Wait a minute, I thought, you're giving me back my *life*?

For three months, we didn't eat until they told us to eat. We slept when they told us. We bathed when they told us. We blinked when they told us.

Another Marine Corps saying, "To err is human; to forgive divine. Neither of which is Marine Corps policy."

They made us think like them, act like them. And now they were cutting us free?

Then I thought, How are we supposed to function without them?

That moment revealed to me the limits of the human mind. Your mind can be swayed, no matter who you are, no matter how tough you think you are.

This also was a lesson the Marines wanted us to learn: Take heed, lest ye fall. Always be aware of your limitations. Always understand the situation that you're in.

In fact, I was one of two Marines out of the seventy women to graduate "with merit." We had one honor marine. She picked up two stripes and became a lance corporal. She was the top, and then there were two of us who graduated with merit and picked up one stripe, or rank.

So there it was. I had graduated. I was no longer a recruit.

I was now Private First Class Earle.

I was a Marine.

* * *

After boot camp, you get a bit of leave to go home. I went back to New York. Everybody was very proud of me. My grandfather had been in the British Army. I was the first of the grandchildren to join the military. I had joined the Marine Corps. After that, several of my cousins joined the military. One joined the Marines as enlisted, and another the Air Force as an officer. He became a helicopter pilot. The dam was broken, and a lot of my family subsequently served.

Most chose their MOS, their military occupational specialty, at the end of boot camp. Not me. I'd signed a contract on recruitment that ensured what my MOS would be.

I'd followed my grandfather Gilbert's advice, "Always have a trade." I'd signed up to become an electrician. I was assigned to Marine Corps Engineer School at Courthouse Bay, Camp Lejeune, North Carolina.

Chapter Seven

THE FEW. THE PROUD.

Engineer School at Courthouse Bay was part of the base at Camp Lejeune. MCES was in the boonies and on the water. That was necessary because Marine engineers must learn how to bring some very large machinery ashore from the ocean. Plus the combat engineers needed a large place to blow things up.

Camp Lejeune takes up 246 square miles. Every base has various functional sectors within it, and every Marine base has an area called Mainside. It's Main Street Downtown where everything starts.

I was slated to join a utilities platoon after graduation. The utilities platoon is part of the Engineers. It's housed in support battalions. The job that I chose, the MOS, as we call it, was MOS 1141. I was the only female in my platoon.

Women Marines are the few, the proud—just like the men. By statute, we could make up only 5 percent of the Corps. In my MOS, it was probably less than a percentage point. Generally, I was the only female around, or one of five or six in larger groups. I am used to being around a lot of men, leading men, and answering to men in authority.

Marines are not subtle. You have to fight for everything you want. You have to fight for your ideas. You can't let yourself be cowed. Marines are a team.

Marines are gentlemen. They will generally attempt to treat you as a woman first, to help with this or that, because that's how they were raised. But I learned that if I let them help me to the extent that society normally required, then I didn't get the respect I needed to get my job done. You have to pull your own weight, otherwise you're of no use to the unit.

You have to dig your own ditch. You can't say, "No, my back hurts." There is no such thing as "can't" in the Marine Corps. Of course, I'd already learned that from growing up in my own family. My grandfather always said, "They need to get rid of this word 'can't' out of the dictionary. There is no such thing as 'can't' in our family." He was Yoda before Yoda was Yoda.

There is only "try," but there is no "I can't do it, so I quit."

The utilities platoon consists of plumbers and electricians. Electricians learned how to design a circuit. We learned how to identify transistors, resistors, and so on. We learned how much of a load you can put on any circuit so that it functions properly, and you don't blow anything or anyone up. You had to learn how to provide electricity for the needs of a field camp or facility, when you go out to the field. That's your main task: to provide electricity while deployed.

How do you do that? You carry with you the mighty mobile power system. It's called an MEP unit. This is a generator, but these are not like Home Depot generators you might buy at the store. They are big one-hundred-kilowatt generators. You have to learn how to hook them up. They run on diesel. You learned to repair them. That's why I also trained as a diesel mechanic.

Because there are many more men and there wasn't individual housing for them, they lived in a squad bay while attending engineers school. Generally women didn't have a whole squad bay. We were really a minority within a minority. And I was even more of a minority because of my MOS.

We were in the Basic Allowance Housing for the enlisted single women. We shared what looked like a hotel room, but there were three of us in it. No privacy, no nothing. I was nineteen and could handle that.

I graduated from engineer school as an 1141, Basic Electrician. (You say it as "Eleven-Forty-one.") I would later return and become an 1142, a Journeyman Electrician.

So I began my job of supplying and maintaining electrical power for the U.S. Marine Corps.

* * *

After training I was assigned to Camp Pendleton, California, 7th Engineers Support Battalion, 1st Field Service Support Group, Charlie Company, Utilities Platoon. In a company there are many different platoons such as utilities, motor transport, supply, communications, and so on. Each platoon has a specialty.

Out to the field I went, practicing deployments and playing war games, but also keeping up equipment maintenance. It was challenging, it was satisfying, and I was good at my job. I felt very much like I'd come of age and was finally entering adulthood full steam.

I remember once we were out in the field at Marine Corps Base Twentynine Palms in California. Our task was to wire a base from scratch out in that desert waste.

It was my job to get the MEP unit up and running. Some Marines from another battalion were hanging around. They didn't know me; I didn't know them. I was very thin back then, a fairly tiny woman. These guys were huge. Some were leaning up against the generator and looking at me rather disdainfully. There was some sneering going on, if you want to know the truth.

I heard one of them ask, "Hey, what is *she* gonna do?"

I walked around the unit. I did my safety check. I flipped this switch, flipped that switch.

The guys were looking at me. Somebody snickered because nothing seemed to be happening.

Now the unit was ready. I pushed a button, flipped another switch, another button. I'm going through and the generator is starting up, she's starting up, and she lets out this rising wail that, if you're nearby, sounds like she's going to blow up.

These big guys take off running as fast as they can. Scattered into the desert.

And I thought to myself, Well, *that's* what she's gonna do.

I'll employ another bit of Marine Corps advice here: "When you've got them by the _ _ _ _ _, their hearts will follow."

* * *

The Marines will either move you up or out. After a certain amount of experience, you are expected to lead. There it was again, another Marine Corps saying, "Either lead, follow, or get the hell out of the way." After a year and a half, my platoon commander decided it was my time, and so I was sent back to North Carolina to journeyman electrician school at MCES.

I went back to Courthouse Bay as a corporal. I saw the newly graduated "boots," as we called them, and felt I'd come a long way. I was only a year and a half out of boot camp, but it felt like much longer. I had picked up two ranks fairly quickly. I was now an NCO—a noncommissioned officer. The next rank—sergeant.

I was now in charge of these boots. There were three platoon classes of electricians and three of plumbers. As a corporal training to be journeyman, at certain times I was expected to take charge of marching the boots at formation.

I'd shout, "Company under my command! Forward march!" And because the company was so big, I'd have to give charge of each platoon to the highest in rank in the platoon. They would march them until we got them to a gathering place, then I could take charge again.

For young people to get that kind of leadership experience is truly amazing. The Marines pushed me to develop in ways I'd never been pushed before.

I returned to Pendleton, where I eventually became a quality control inspector after making journeyman electrician. I was one of several responsible for ensuring that all power units were properly repaired, so I inspected what the other electricians had done. Our platoon would have five or six women by the time I left.

Mostly, the Marines were males. Couldn't let that bother me. I had to run clean up behind them: "Fix this, do this, do this."

I just had to get it done.

* * *

The Marine Corps uniform means something. The Eagle, Globe, and Anchor are important. That's our shibboleth. If you don't know how to say the order of our emblem, then you're not a Marine. It's pumped into you from boot camp. When you become a Marine, you've accomplished something major in life.

Women were not allowed in combat during my time, which meant a WM's opportunities overseas at the time were limited. There were differences in qualifications for the sexes. We didn't have to run as far, and so on. But, believe me, we had to run. A *lot*. The requirements were adapted. But when it came to shooting, oh no, everybody had to qualify.

I did have an opportunity to go to Okinawa, but those orders came down in such a way you were allowed to refuse them. I opted to stay stateside. I'm sorry I did that. I was in love at the time. So stupid of me!

Generally female Marines at the time didn't get to go very many places. Male Marines who wore at least one row of ribbons had *done* something. The Marine Corps doesn't give out medals easily.

But a Marine is a Marine. The basic skills remain constant across the sexes. Cleaning weapons. Qualifying. Playing war games. Setting up tents. Digging holes. Having to practice keeping one eye open and one eye closed so you don't lose your night vision if the enemy sends up a flare.

You are a rifleman first, last, and always.

When I got out of boot camp, my first duty station was California Camp Pendleton. I was in my BAQ fast asleep and suddenly I awakened boom, boom, boom. I was thinking for a second, Oh my God, it's World War III and we are being attacked! But this was Marine big guns firing. We were playing war games. It was so close, everything was shaking. Many a night I woke up to that.

Our battalion would engage in war games often, as well. I'd find myself out in the Twentynine Palms desert. During the day you're burning your buttocks off, and then at night you're freezing your buttocks off. When you go to bed and you're a rookie, the old-timers tell you to take your poncho and you throw it over yourself because if you don't in the morning, you'll have a mouthful of sand. The wind just blows and blows and blows. Other times I was out there figuring out what leaf to use for certain situations. You're simulating war conditions. This is real stuff, and weapons are *always* involved.

We were the first generation to have Meals—Ready to Eat, or MREs. My platoon in boot camp was the last one to eat C-rats. This was when your food came in cans. Then we went over to MREs, and that first generation of MREs, let me tell you, still had some kinks to work out. It would give you the runs like nobody's business. The best MRE meal was the spaghetti and meatballs, but even that gave you the runs. When you got C-rats, you were issued a John Wayne—a little can opener, very utilitarian. You could put it on your key ring. It also served as a screwdriver. You can always tell people who were in the military up to that point because we all know what a John Wayne is.

Once the guys caught a snake and I watched them roast the thing.

The MREs were done. We just could *not* eat them anymore. I told myself no, I'm not eating snake. Well, after a while you'll eat just about anything. They're roasting and roasting. I'm eyeing it. It has this white flesh. It didn't look too...snakey. They're enjoying it. So I ask, "What does it taste like?"

"Taste like chicken."

"Well then give me some, then!"

I ate snake. They were right. It was soft. Tasted just like chicken.

Another time they caught deer, roasted that. We threw some hot sauce on and it was the best meat I ever tasted. Quite nice.

Another time we were out in the boonies playing war games. We had agreed on what the password would be. Our battalion was warring with the other. We were told that when we saw the green flare shoot up, that meant we were overrun, that we in our platoons were on our own.

Then, wouldn't you know it, ten minutes into the fight our battalion throws up the green flare. Our headquarters were instantly captured.

What? Why? Everybody was on the horn trying to figure out what was going on.

This is why you have war games. You have to practice. It turned out nobody could remember the password sequence! We had accidentally given the enemy the password instead of the challenge. We were doomed from the start!

In the real world, you die if you do something like that. That's why you practice constantly. You debrief. You improve.

Speaking of war games brings to mind another Marine Corps saying, "When you are up to your _ _ _ in alligators, it is difficult to remind yourself that your initial objective was to drain the swamp."

Interesting times.

We were warriors. That was the business we were in.

* * *

During this time, I was becoming an adult in more ways than one.

I got pregnant.

This happened during my first hitch at Pendleton. By the time I returned to MCES for journeyman electrician school, I had had a daughter.

I named her DeJon.

How did this happen? The usual way, of course. Emotionally, I guess I was still reeling from my grandmother's death and I wanted someone to love. Somewhere in the back of my mind, perhaps I thought a baby would do it.

I was not married. He wanted me to marry him; I said no. We parted ways, and I moved on.

I had one babysitter for DeJon during my time in the Marines. She loved her and spoiled her rotten. When I would pick my daughter up from the babysitter, I could hardly put her down because she was so used to being cradled.

I had a month off after DeJon's birth, then I had to return to work. The Marine Corps is like any other job in this way. You come to work daily. Then it's not like any other job, and you might be on mission for days or weeks without coming home.

* * *

I became a U.S. citizen when I was in the Corps. As a matter of fact, I was pregnant at the time. I made that decision, studied, and was brought before the judge in San Diego. He asked question after question about U.S. history, government, and so on. He asked about the courts. I got through it and I raised my right hand.

I was serving in the Armed Forces of the United States. I'd had a child who was a U.S. citizen. I might return to Jamaica to visit, and I would always be a Jamaican by heritage, but I knew in my heart I was an American for life. I was already willing to give my life for the country. Look at the Naturalization Oath of Allegiance. This says it all.

I hereby declare, on oath, that I absolutely and entirely renounce and abjure all allegiance and fidelity to any foreign prince, potentate, state, or sovereignty, of whom or which I have heretofore been a subject or citizen; that I will support and defend the Constitution and laws of the United States of America against all enemies, foreign and domestic; that I will bear true faith and allegiance to the same; that I will bear arms on behalf of the United States when required by the law; that I will perform noncombatant service in the Armed Forces of the United States when required by the law; that I will perform work of national importance under civilian direction when required by the law.[1]

When I went to get my U.S. passport photo, I was wearing my Marine Corps uniform. I didn't know I wasn't allowed to wear a military uniform in a passport photo. Here in America, the military doesn't run the country. We obey civilian rule.

I had to throw the photographer's filthy smock over me.

But I loved my new American passport. The American passport is an achievement for immigrants. It's the golden ticket. People sacrifice everything to get one.

America. What a country!

I became a naturalized citizen October 25, 1984, at the U.S. District Court near Pendleton.

*　*　*

I was twenty-two when I had DeJon. I was still a child myself in some ways.

Being a single parent and a Marine is very difficult. I began to feel I was not being fair to the Marine Corps. There were times I couldn't be deployed because I couldn't find anyone to look after DeJon. This distressed me greatly. When you are a Marine, letting down your fellow Marines in any way is a *big deal*.

The Marine Corps saved my life. It gave me structure and purpose at a time in my life when both had been blasted away by my grandmother's death. There were times I hated it because it was hard. But there is no camaraderie like it anywhere else. When, for example, our babies were born, we Marines would buy cigars, shove a stogie in everybody's mouth, and I was there smoking with the guys. It didn't matter that I was female.

Whenever care packages arrived with cookies and good stuff, the platoon shared in the bounty. We all ate Mom's cookies together. Whenever the guys were going out to some club or other, they'd stop by my BHQ.

"Hey, Earle, you wanna come?"

"Yes!"

And we'd all pile into a car. We weren't male or female. We were just Marines. Black or White. Asian or Latino. We left all that stuff behind. That was for other people to worry about. And we were all so young.

Just a few months ago, I was honored at Marine Corps Barracks 8th and I, an ancient U.S. Marine Corps garrison in Washington, DC.

After it was over, we went to the O Club (the Officer's Club). Now you have to understand, as enlisted I would not have been allowed within a mile of the O Club. There was no fraternization in the Marine Corps. My husband was with us. He is a retired Marine Corps officer. So we went in to finish up the night.

Turns out the officers were just like the enlisted. They like having fun, too, regular folks. You don't see that side of the officers as enlisted. Oh no, it's spit and polish and shine.

But now we understood each other and we were one. That's how it feels. You're one. One body. One purpose. One mind. Team is what matters. And we look out for one another. And if you hurt one of us... well, the rest of us are coming for you. That's just how it is.

Finally there was yet another deployment coming up, and I was forced to beg off because it came at a time my babysitter was entirely unavailable and I had no family member to come and stay with her, or anyplace I could leave her on short notice.

It just was not going to work. I had one more year left on my enlistment, yet I felt that I was not pulling my weight. You have to pull your weight when you're a Marine. You have to be part of the team. There are no excuses.

After a day of anguish, I came to a decision.

I petitioned for an early out.

Days, and then weeks, passed and I heard nothing.

I kept going to work.

One day I was out in the yard setting up a three-kilowatt generator. This was a smaller generator, but heavy enough to require several people to lift it if a forklift is unavailable. We were moving it from one side of a site to another.

As usual, I was surrounded by guys, and I had an easy rapport with all of them. We were a team. We even kidded around.

We'd agreed that, on the count of three, we were going to lift.

The guys decided to play a prank on me. There were six of us, three on one side and three on the other. We were always playing tricks on each other. I suppose when your organization's ultimate purpose involves war, levity helps.

We counted. We all grunted, "Lift!"

I lifted; they didn't.

"Guys!"

The generator didn't budge. The guys burst out laughing at their little prank.

I heard a pop in my back. Something didn't feel right after that.

That night it was hard to walk. By the next day, it wasn't better, so I went to sick bay to have it checked out. They couldn't find anything immediately wrong.

Not long afterward, I found out I had been granted my early out. I was leaving active duty in the Marine Corps.

When I was granted the early out, I had only one week's notice. Apparently the request had long been granted, but had never come down the pike. This was the proverbial situation where your paperwork gets lost and nobody knows that it was approved, so you don't have time to plan your exit.

I was not prepared. My platoon leader had assumed it had *not* been granted and I was about to leave on another deployment. I received a call two days before that deployment asking why I had not completed my medical discharge appointment.

I went for the medical exam for discharge and saw that my back injury was already listed in my SRB, Service Record Book, and it was noted in my medical records that I had suffered this injury. Though it wasn't manifesting too badly, I did hurt myself in the Corps. At the time, I thought little of this, but that notation proved very important. The injury worsened and nearly destroyed my life a few years later. But I don't want to get ahead of myself.

In Corps life there's such camaraderie. You get close to your fellow Marines. We understand one another. We're a breed apart.

This felt as if it would be suddenly taken from me. I did not have the normal opportunity to wind down. Most Marines knew long in advance when their time would be done. There were traditions to help us cope.

With my sudden departure looming, I didn't have time to situate myself. I wasn't going to get all the normal celebrations that occur when you're about to leave the Corps. In the Marines, they ask, "How short are you?" You indicate a small distance from the ground with a hand motion and answer, "I'm this short." Or you answer, "Fifteen days and a wake-up," something like that. I didn't get those little things.

I got, *Bam, you're out.*

I had to get my medical done quickly. Everything was very rushed. I entered the service in a shocked state, you could say, because of what

I experienced with my grandmother, and I left in a shocked state. They had become my family.

And I had two days to get ready to leave it behind.

Those days came and went. I had been active in the Marine Corps three years and three months. Yet I knew, as other Marines do, that I was a Marine for life.

"Once a Marine, always a Marine." Yet another Marine Corps saying.

Chapter Eight

THE REPUBLICAN ROAD

I once asked my husband, "What would have happened if you had met me while I was still in the Marine Corps?"

This would have been extremely unlikely. Camp Pendleton is simply huge. He was stationed out in the boonies during his time there. I was Mainside. Oh, at times the battalions fight with each other in war games. I guess it *could* have happened.

He replied, "No question. I would never have risked my career for you."

I know he was telling the truth. He was an officer. I was enlisted. It's just not done. Well, hardly ever. It's frowned upon.

* * *

DeJon and I spent a year alone in California. I took some time to figure out what moves I wanted to make. Was I going to stay in California, or was I going to go back to New York? I didn't go back to Jamaica that year, either. I stayed put. We lived off my savings until my job in sales came through. We were in an apartment in Vista, California, maybe twenty minutes from the back gate at Pendleton.

During that time, I'd joined a club to meet people, to get myself out. These are not uncommon around military bases to help us get back into civilian life. There is a transition, and it's difficult sometimes because we speak a different language in the Marines. You have to find a way to ease back into civilian society once you muster out.

I went to a few get-togethers and had female friends in the group. One lady's name was Katia. One day, Katia cornered me at a meetup and said, "Hey, there's this guy. He's seen your photo and he wants to talk."

I nodded, not giving my assent just yet.

"Okay. Can you tell me anything else?"

"He's a Marine officer. I know that."

I laughed. Oh no! Definitely not. Marine officers...

"What's his rank?"

"I think...lieutenant maybe?"

"First or second?"

"I don't know...maybe second?"

Oh no. A butterbar!

I wasn't ready for that. I let Katia know.

But she said, "No, no, he's a nice guy. I would never have recommended him otherwise."

She went on for a bit, and after a while I acquiesced.

"Okay, fine. One date, but that's it."

Later, Terry and I thought Katia had such a beautiful name, we named our first child together after her.

* * *

Second Lieutenant Terence (Terry) Sears called me not long after, and I let him know I was tired. He told me that was fine, we could just watch a movie.

I *was* tired. I'd been working all day.

He came over. I don't remember much. I was on the couch. We talked.

I wanted to gauge his character.

But I ended up thinking, Well, he's not so bad.

I didn't mention that I had been in the Corps. What I failed to remember as I showed him a photo album was that my own Marine Corps photos were in there.

"Oh, so you are a Marine?"

We laughed. Watched the movie. The next thing I knew, I woke from falling fast asleep.

He was walking out the door.

I exclaimed, "Oh, I'm sorry! The movie's over!"

He smiled. "I was just going to let myself out."

I thought to myself, This guy's not so bad. He's being great about this. He'd brought over white zinfandel and flowers, and here I went falling asleep on the man.

So I told him, "Okay, I owe you a real date. I did tell you I was very tired before you came over, however."

The very next day, he brought over more flowers and more wine. Now, I don't normally drink wine and I hate flowers. If you want to give me something, give me a plant. Flowers die right away. What good is that? Nowadays, he buys me a flowering plant when he wants to give me something special. You get to know somebody after thirty-seven years.

Way led on to way, and we were soon married. As Diana Ross once said, instead of looking at the past, I put myself ahead twenty years and look at myself and try to imagine what I need to do now to get there then.[1] It was perhaps the wisest and best decision I ever made.

Terry adopted DeJon as his own. She was a year going on two at the time. He became her father, the only father that she ever knew.

* * *

Terry and I had our babies rather quickly. We got married and we had our first child together, Katia, and I got pregnant again six months later.

I was selling life insurance at that point part-time in a commission-based job with Surety Life Insurance, a Sears affiliate.

I went out selling policies when I could. I was extremely pregnant with Janel when I landed what was to be a big account. I would wait for my husband to come home, and he would take care of the babies and I would walk neighborhoods and put the company's palm cards and leaflets underneath the doors of businesses.

My idea was to get in with an employer as a one-stop solution for his workers. One evening, I was working the commercial district of Carlsbad, California. It was late at night. Here I was, very pregnant. I finished putting a card under a door, and I turned to see a police car. He followed along after me for a bit, probably wondering what this pregnant woman was doing. After a while I guess he was satisfied I was not up to no good, and he smiled, nodded, and drove away.

I later got a call on one of those cards, and that was my big first sell for Surety. It just goes to show you that if you want to get something done you really have to pull out all the stops. I was out there at nine o'clock at night drumming up business. It helps that I happen to like sales.

The same day, I was on my way to another appointment. I was wearing high heels. I don't know what I was doing in those high heels being so pregnant, but I got that particular tremor women often get, and I almost tripped. By this time I knew what it meant. Sure enough, within a day or two Janel, my third baby, was born.

I almost died having Janel. I had asked my doctor for an epidural when I had Katia because I was in such pain. He refused! When I got pregnant again, I said to him I'm going to want an epidural this time, and if you don't think you can give me one, let me know now and I will find another OB/GYN.

Well, I got my epidural, but it wasn't helping that much. I was in labor at the hospital and suddenly I felt myself sinking and losing consciousness. It was like one of those hospital television shows when the doors bust open and in fly the nurses and the doctors. Everything was dim to me. All I heard were shouts of "We're losing her," and "We're losing the baby." Terry was there as well, and when I saw his eyes pop wide, I knew I was in danger. He's normally imperturbable. Furthermore, I was losing consciousness.

Someone put an oxygen mask over my face and they started moving the baby around.

Someone else said, "We can't get a heartbeat on the baby; the baby's in trouble."

They were about to do a C-section when suddenly everything *switched*. I came out of it, regained consciousness, and started feeling better.

You guessed it, the umbilical cord had been wrapped around Janel's neck. Then it was time to have the baby, so I gave natural birth to Janel.

My mother came up from Jamaica to help me, as she had with the other children.

This time, my mother gazed at me very seriously and said, "This is the last baby."

Well, I wasn't having that. I told her my husband and I would decide on such matters, thank you very much.

She shook her head and said, "No, this is the last baby."

And indeed, Janel *was* my last baby.

Janel and Katia were born at Vista Hospital in California. DeJon had been born at the Naval Hospital Camp Pendleton. Janel was born jaundiced, poor thing, and I had to take her to the doctor for a time after she was born until she got better. DeJon, I'd almost lost. She had trouble moderating her temperature at first. They had to keep her under a heating light. I prayed, "Lord, don't tell me I brought her all this way only to lose her."

Thankfully, she recovered.

After Katia was born, I sold insurance. I continued for a while, but after Janel, I figured the best thing would be something that came with a salary and was close by. I had three children now under four. I got a job as the assistant branch manager at a bank in Carlsbad, California. I'd never been in banking, but they hired me.

Terry was still in the Marines during this time. He'd been promoted to first lieutenant. He was a motor transport officer. He was at Pendleton, but as I've noted, Pendleton is huge, and he was out in the boonies.

I went to work thinking this would perhaps be the start of my new career.

But at the end of that week the new babysitter said to me that Janel was not adjusting to her, that she cried all day.

The next week the babysitter told me, "She's not thriving; this is not going to work. The baby needs you."

She was an Indian American woman, older. I could sense she knew what she was talking about. With us younger mothers, sometimes we don't realize. I thank God for her.

"Mama, this baby is not thriving, you've got to stay home. She needs you."

So that was it. The babysitter was willing to lose three children at one time. Whereas the other two were fine with my being outside the home, Janel was not. Terry and I talked and decided that it was better for me to stay home, and that was what I did.

Early the next year, with his growing family to support, Terry came to another decision. By that time, I'd also experienced an internal revolution of my own.

*   *   *

Janel came along during the 1988 presidential campaign, which featured Michael Dukakis versus George H. W. Bush. This was the end of the Reagan years. If Bush won, the thought was it would be in some ways Reagan's third term.

At the time, I was no fan of Ronald Reagan. When you're surrounded by a lot of Democrats it's hard to see outside the bubble. My
father wasn't a Democrat, he was more of a political independent, but
when you live in the Black community in New York, they're all Democrats. You hear nothing but bad about Republicans.

So I assumed that I was a Democrat. I'd never voted at that point,
but I figured, well, I'm Black. I'm *supposed* to be Democrat. Who told
me? Nobody and everybody. That's what Black people did, wasn't it?

I was at home with the girls not long after Janel was born. It was
the political season leading up to the national election of 1988. Television was filled with political commercials. I was watching one after
another as I cared for the kids. Michael Dukakis in his commercial
said he was going to expand abortion, that he was going to increase
taxes. Furthermore, he was going to expand the government welfare
program and other government programs.

I thought: *Wait.* Wait one minute here. I don't believe in *any* of
that.

Then right behind Dukakis, Bush aired his commercials.

"I will reduce abortion."

Now that sat well with me because I'd just had my baby three
months prior.

Bush went on to say, "I'm going to *reduce* your taxes."

I thought, that's excellent, I'm cheap! Well, the kids call me cheap.
I like to think of it as *frugal*. Reduce my taxes!

Then he said something that blew my mind, and it was the political
turning point of my life. I'll never forget it.

"If all you ever have is welfare, you will never have anything to pass
on to your children."

I felt my soul agreeing with him. It is our duty to do *more* for our
children. With welfare, we possess only up to the limits of the government's checks. Dependence and an impoverished life will follow.

Sitting there surrounded by my girls, saving and scrimping to make ends meet, my husband and I working to give them a good life, a better life than even we had had, I couldn't agree more.

I said to myself, "Oh, my God. I'm a Republican."

Before that, I didn't know, hadn't realized.

That is why I so strongly believe that Republicans must never concede the vote of any group, or race, or ethnic background to anyone. Republicans must make the case to *everyone*. It is our *duty*. I'm not saying all Black people should become Republicans. No! I very much want political freedom.

Black people deserve the truth. It's going to take time and money and effort. In majority Black countries, Black people are on both sides of the political spectrum and everything is better.

* * *

We knew we didn't want to be so far away from family forever. Terry thought we might go to South Dakota where he'd spent his childhood and gone to college, but I told him I couldn't do South Dakota. Too cold.

He was disappointed. All his friends were there. He'd been there since he was a little child after his parents came back from Okinawa, Japan, where his father had been stationed after he was in Vietnam. His father had been a journalist in the Air Force. His mom and dad had married early. Both were from Norfolk, Virginia.

Terry comes from a large family on his father's side. His dad was the oldest grandchild. My husband's great-grandmother on his father's side was still having children when her children began having children, so his father, as the oldest grandchild, had to call two of his aunts "aunt" even though he was older than they were.

Terry's father was stationed in Minot, North Dakota, but the family lived in South Dakota. He went to Catholic school from middle school to high school. He was the middle child, the only boy. He went to South Dakota State. He was going to apply for Air Force ROTC, but, as Terry puts it, he partied a little bit too much. The nuns hadn't sent in his paperwork properly. He wasn't on the ball, so he missed his chance.

At that point, Terry's father read him the riot act. He told him he'd better buckle down. He made him work his way through college. I think the family helped somewhat still, but my husband learned the hard way!

He paid for college, graduated, then joined the Marine Corps and went straight to officer candidate school.

Terry didn't have any Marines in the family. Most of his uncles had gone into the Army as officers. His family is a very educated family. It was education, of course, that lifted them out of poverty. Education again and again made the difference. They were Black, coming up during the civil rights movement and before. Some had been veterans. Out of the fifteen children that his grandmother had, thirteen of them had college degrees in various fields. That's a Black family in the South. Think about that. Education lifts us up.

My political relationship with Terry's family has had its ups and downs.

I decided to run for the House of Delegates, which is Virginia's version of the U.S. House of Representatives (although Virginia's came first and was the inspiration for the national version!). Two of Terry's family members took out an ad against me in the Black newspaper serving the Hampton Roads–Newport News area, and *for* my opponent.

My opponent did not let that go unnoticed.

Twenty years later, after I was elected lieutenant governor of Virginia, I asked Terry's cousin (this time on his father's side), retired judge Richard Taylor, to swear me in.

So our family is not unusual in having political differences. On my side there are also issues, and I have a cousin or two who won't speak to me because of politics. I have friends who have left because of politics. Oh, how I wish we could let each other be!

* * *

The Marines were going through a reduction in force in the late 1980s and we had such a young family. After some soul searching, Terry made the call and decided not to stay in. We remained in California for another year after Janel was born, and he went to work for Goodyear.

I wanted to get back to the East Coast. I was tired of living so far from family. But I didn't want to go back to New York. I knew that New York was not the place for my young family. I didn't think it was conducive to a healthy life for toddlers. I'd been advised by some of my cousins not to come back, that it was better to find somewhere else.

South Dakota was out.

So where?

One day Terry said, "Hey, I've got family in Virginia. We could go there and live."

I was still very much a New Yorker at the time. I replied, "You mean out in the country? Live in the *sticks*?"

He answered with a chuckle, "Virginia's nice. It's quite populated and civilized, you know."

We moved to Virginia in 1989. Terry's grandmother on his mother's side lived in Portsmouth, and we moved in with her for a time. Then we found our own house in Larchmont in Norfolk. We bought there because it was close to Old Dominion University.

I had determined that it was high time I got a college education. After all, I'd promised my grandmother I would. Furthermore, I wanted to become a lawyer, my childhood dream.

I didn't start there, but at Tidewater Community College. Depending on where classes were being held, I went to either the Virginia

Beach campus or the Portsmouth campus. It was cheaper, and I noticed that many of the same professors who taught at ODU also taught at Tidewater, so why pay a higher price for it? We were living on one income. After I got an associate's degree at Tidewater, I moved on to ODU.

I was utterly determined to finish college, almost to the exclusion of all else. Living in Larchmont, I wouldn't need a full-time babysitter. Terry would come home from work and I would be able to go to school, and I could go other times during the day with daycare for the kids, depending on classes.

Terry had transferred from Goodyear in California to Newport News. I would take the kids to daycare, and then I went to school. I was twenty-six when I started. I had three children under five when I began to take classes. The first two years of college, I'm afraid I don't remember my children's lives so well because I was in class so much. I was taking eighteen hours, twenty hours even. I went during summers. I was simply in school the whole time.

We had to sell one of our cars to make ends meet. I rode my husband's bicycle to school (which was another reason we had to be close). I finished college in three years. We had very little money, but we had a plan. I was going to finish college and go to law school.

Why?

I'd always wanted to be a lawyer. At least, so I told myself. In Jamaica, we were constantly talking politics, and I wanted to go into politics from a young age. To do that, I needed to be a lawyer, right?

So I decided to become one. I didn't want to be forty and wonder "What if?" What would have happened if I'd just done what I dreamed of doing? I wanted to *actually experience* my dreams. I felt that I was already old. Here I was doing college the nontraditional way.

I'm not sure where I got the idea, but I decided the way I would be getting into politics would be as a staff professional, helping politicians run their organizations, writing their speeches, running campaigns.

This remained my goal for years. I later went to campaign manager's school, not candidate's school. I never particularly wanted to *be* the politician. I wanted to be the person behind the politician. But God had other plans.

Since I wanted to go to law school, I was advised to major in English at ODU. I intended to specialize in international law, because of my Jamaica connection. I wanted to argue before the international courts. Where I got that idea, go figure.

I was advised, however, that since lawyers have to prove so many points and make so many arguments that the best thing would be to get an English degree. So I did, and I *hated* it. I had to write a paper every week, sometimes two or three! I had to do so much research. I decided that all that work ought to at least lead to something concrete, so I got an English degree concentrating in journalism. That was my major.

I needed a minor, and I chose economics. I soon began to love economics so much that I considered becoming a journalist focused on the business side of things, the economic side of things. I considered getting a double major in English and economics, but that would've meant an extra year in school. It might look good on my résumé, but that would have been another year of my life, and I was already starting college late—at least that was the way I saw it at the time. I do sometimes wish I had an economics major. I very much enjoyed it as my minor subject.

* * *

I had an interesting source of income during this time, as well.

Throughout college, one way that we survived with just one income was by my selling cars. I would regularly comb through the *Auto Trader* magazine. At the time a private person could sell up to six cars per year in Virginia without a business license.

That was what I did. I would buy cars very cheaply and sell them much higher, at least double what I paid. Terry would inspect the cars to make sure they were mechanically sound and then I would deal with all negotiations.

One time I bought a vehicle from a retired Army officer—I think he was a colonel—and I bargained with him really hard. We finally agreed upon a price, and he said to me, "After we sign the paperwork, if you see I have any other cars to sell... *don't* call me."

I would make anywhere between $2,000 to $3,000 each sell. It was pretty good money, times six cars a year. I know how to negotiate; my husband knows if a car is good or not. I'm a salesperson at heart—or an extrovert at heart, at least. I like talking to people.

You've heard the old saying "That's a person who never met a stranger"? That's me. I'm a very outgoing person. Of course, I wasn't really looking for interaction at the time. I needed money!

I'd buy the *Auto Trader* or I'd look through the classifieds in the local papers. I'd narrow it down. I'd go look at a few cars and the one that I figured would bring in the most money, I bought. I could do especially well when all the car needed was to be cleaned on the inside. Plus, I'd wash the darn thing. So much of life is about presentation, so much of life is about showing up looking decent and ready to go.

If someone wanted to sell his car as is, I'd have a look. My husband would check and if he told me there was nothing wrong with it, okay, I would buy it—and turn around and sell it for $2,000 to $3,000 profit or more. The seller could've gotten the same amount, but he didn't put in the work, so I did. I know a good deal when I see one.

I didn't continue doing this long after college. Flipping used cars worked for me in the moment, but my husband grew tired of it. I considered that maybe we could have bought a car dealership or done something similar, but he didn't want to do that *at all*. He'd had enough with motor transportation in the Marines, perhaps.

I liked the idea of starting our own business. I like to take risks. That's what I do. I've never had any experience in anything that I've been hired to do. If I'm already working someplace, it behooves me—and I even feel it's incumbent upon me—to make myself indispensable.

I would advise this to everyone, to young folks particularly. Life isn't going to wait for you. It never does. Life—meaningful activity—doesn't just happen; you have to help make it happen. You do that by being useful, good at what you do, whatever that is. I know it sounds a bit cynical, a little cold, but that's it. Life waits for no one; either you are ready or you are not.

* * *

I was a Republican in college, and I didn't care who knew. I have never lied about or tried to hide my political beliefs. On the contrary, they inform who I am and what I do. If I'm following the bidding of the Lord, why conceal this? Instead, I try to live in the light of His will.

Having been raised in Jamaica where there is the right and the left, I don't see why I have to justify my political leanings. I am what I choose to be in the same way others are who they choose to be politically. I know that Black people should be in all areas of the political spectrum. We have nothing to prove.

Anyway, I was steadily marching toward my goal. I was finally getting my bachelor's. Along the way ODU's career department helped me secure an internship with the Norfolk Southern railroad. Their headquarters was in downtown Norfolk. I worked in their labor relations department. It was a paid internship, which was wonderful because it brought money in. My job was to summarize various court decisions from the National Labor Relations Board.

Wow, was I bored.

I was bored with the legalese. I was bored with everything about the law. I started rethinking if this was really what I wanted to do. Did I want to become a lawyer? Because it just seemed *stifling*. I was buried in paperwork and research.

I don't really get to see anybody, to interact with people, I thought.

What did I really like about the law, anyway? I liked arguing and proving my point. After that, the rest of it was not so interesting.

Yet I plodded along, dead set on becoming a lawyer. A lawyer practicing international law. It was a shining image in my mind, but I really had no idea what it meant.

I passed the LSAT. And low and behold, I got accepted to George Mason University School of Law.

* * *

George Mason is in Fairfax, Virginia, near Washington, DC. That is three and a half hours away from where we lived. It was time to finally sit down with myself and make a decision. To attend law school, I would have to pick up the whole family again to move them. My husband would have to leave his job and find another. There was no way that I could just go away to school alone and return on weekends and holidays.

We talked it over again and again.

I had very young children. The family must stay together.

I took out the yellow legal pad and I listed the pros and cons. We call these "come-to-Jesus moments," those times when the rubber hits the road and you ask yourself the "why" questions.

Why do I really want to become a lawyer?

Number one, I'll never forget, was to show my father that I could do it. I wanted him to be proud of me.

Number two, so that my mother could say her daughter was a lawyer.

Number three, to make lots of money.

Number four...well, I don't remember. I only remember number six.

Number six was to help people.

I looked at my list and I could go no further. I realized I was fooling myself. The only reason I'd ever *said* I wanted to become a lawyer was to help people. But it was now number six.

If my heart wasn't in it, then would I ever make it? Did I even have the passion for this?

All in all, it just wasn't going to work.

I wrote to George Mason and thanked them for accepting me, but said that I would not be coming.

It was the right thing to do, but I felt so frustrated. It was maddening to know I had a calling, a strong calling, to do...well, something.

But what could it be?

What was I *missing*?

The answer was on its way, and when it arrived, it would transform my life completely.

What I was missing was God.

Chapter Nine

SPEAKING GOD'S BLESSINGS

The last year that we were in California we were living in a condo. We had a downstairs neighbor who came knocking on our door one day and asked if she could take our children to church.

I thought, Well, that's unusual. Does she have an ulterior motive? But I'd seen her often and I knew she was a perfectly good person. She was not being pushy. She was sincere.

I also thought about how I'd grown up in church, and now my children weren't going to church. I knew that they should be there, but I was far away from God at the time. Here was someone who I knew had decent intentions.

After some deliberation, I said yes. I got them ready for her to take. Sunday came and they were wearing big bows and shiny shoes, and off my two oldest went with her. When they came back, they were full of joy and they were talking about this and that. They showed me their coloring. She asked if they might come next Sunday. The following Sunday, I got them ready and sent them off again. As I was getting them ready, I grew irritated with myself. This is my job, and I hadn't done it. I was supposed to be introducing them to God.

My husband had been a Catholic growing up. He was even a

former altar and choir boy. But he was not practicing by then. Neither of us went to church. So when my neighbor brought them back from Sunday school the second time, I told her that I wanted to go with her the following Sunday.

The following week, I got all three of the girls ready, and we all went to church. We kept it up. My husband at that point came along a couple of times, but he wasn't too keen on it.

We'd established a routine, but it was broken once we left California and came to Virginia. We didn't go to church for about a year.

I recall one Sunday morning the following summer. I was sitting on the sofa playing solitaire and watching television. Janel, the baby, was learning to walk by toddling around our place. She was wearing only a diaper at the time because it was so hot. We had a storm door that was half screen at the top, with the bottom tempered glass. Janel was standing at the glass portion of the storm door and leaning on it looking out the front door.

The sun lined up with the door. I glanced over at a flash of white, and what I saw held my gaze. The light streaming through seemed to illuminate Janel from within, and the sunlight surrounded her with an aura.

I very distinctly heard a voice say, "She is going to grow up not knowing Me and she is going to blame you."

I was suddenly filled with a feeling of panic. It was one thing for *me* not to be in a good relationship with God, but to think I would be held responsible for never introducing my daughter to God was unbearable. How could she decide if there is a God, how could she worship the Creator of her own free will if she never even knew about Him?

That I could not have on my conscience.

That week I set about trying to find a church to attend. The following Sunday I went to a church nearby. It seemed to me a maintaining church, a place where everyone was set in what they thought and didn't feel the need to express the basic faith. All form, without the substance I was seeking for my daughters. I didn't *have* anything to maintain. My relationship with God had pretty much ended when I was twelve years old.

The Sunday after that, I visited another church. This one seemed dead to me. There seemed to be no inner life manifesting there. It was stultifying. I went to another the following week. More of the same.

Wow, I thought, it can't be this difficult!

Not long after, I was at a children's playground not far from my home. Another mom was there with her kids. She and I got to talking, and I asked her where she went to church. Was it close by?

She said, no, it's not close, it's in Newport News. Then she thought a moment and said, you know, I visited a church recently with a young pastor. He comes on local TV sometimes, too. I really felt something there. If I were going to choose a church right now, that's where I would go.

This seemed like a good endorsement, so I watched the pastor on television the following Sunday. He was a young man. During his sermon, I heard him say, "If you are shacking up this is *not* the church for you." This particularly struck me. There were so many pastors and preachers who were all about the soft side of Christianity. This seemed to me a false interpretation of Jesus' words of forgiveness. For them, nothing was verboten, everything was to be tolerated. Let's all just marinate in our sin and smile about it like everything's fine.

I could hardly believe a pastor was talking about personal responsibility. He wasn't putting the fault on society, either.

This man was down-to-earth, no nonsense. The following Sunday I listened again, and was impressed once more. I thought, I don't know where he's getting his wisdom from, he's so young. How can he know these things? I'm going to go see this person.

So I went to Calvary Revival on my own. This was the message and the church I'd been seeking. I eventually got to know more of the pastor's story. He was married, with four children. He was from Tennessee. He'd gone to MIT and met his wife while in Boston. After graduating, he went to work and was making a good salary when he felt the Lord call him to be a pastor.

As many men and women of God have done before, he left it all to follow his calling. His wife, Janeen, told the congregation that they were so poor at one point that their daughter had wanted an ice cream cone from McDonald's and they couldn't afford it.

I wondered, Who is this God that a man could pick up and leave a promising career, a wealthy life, based on a voice, a calling?

Courtney McBath was adamant that a person could not be a part of any ministry in this church until he or she had gone through new members class where he or she was taught principles. For example: What are angels? What do they do? Who is this God and what does He want? What is tithing? What is your role in the church? What is the Bible about?

It was the basics of Christianity. And I needed to hear them.

Evangelical Christians call this "being discipled." After you are discipled, then you are to disciple someone else. It's a mentorship. This was foundational Christianity, but I'd never encountered it in its pure form before. It was exactly what I needed.

McBath started Calvary Revival Church with about fifty people. These days it's got around eight thousand to ten thousand members. But you couldn't push a broom in that church until you had been discipled. He didn't care if you were a pastor from somewhere else and you wanted to be a member. Everybody's got to go through new member's class.

He invited us to question, to find answers. For example, we discussed the biblical teaching on tithing. Now putting money in the offering plate had always been a prickly subject with me. I have been known to make change out of an offering plate.

But as McBath was teaching on tithing, I finally understood the principle of Christian giving.

"Are you saying that I have to give *ten percent* of what I earn to the church?"

"Yes, it's right there in the Bible."

"Ten percent? What are y'all doing with the money? That's a lot of money!"

He said, "Well, we've got to keep the lights on. We've got to pay for the heat and the AC. We've got to expand. Got to pay the mortgage. You like the seats you're sitting in, I take it?"

I still thought it was a tremendous amount to expect. Ten percent of our income? Come on!

I asked, "Is that gross, or is that net?"

He answered, "Tell me, do you want to be blessed by God on the gross or on the net?"

This was still sitting uneasily with me. Ten percent!

I asked, "How do we know that the money is going to be spent properly?"

He laughed and said, "There's one in every crowd."

Yes, I'm often that *one* in the crowd who asks the hard questions nobody else wants to.

He continued, "Sister Sears, your money isn't enough for me to go to hell over. We have the Evangelical Council for Accounting, an independent evangelical auditing organization, and every year they audit our books. We invite them in."

Tithing was a big stretch for us. But we did it. And we have not regretted it. God has been faithful. God says that He is not going to make Himself indebted to us. In that first year we had given around a thousand—which was a shock to our finances. We were still baby Christians.

I generally balanced the family checkbook. But later that year, in

November or December as I recall, there seemed to be an extra $1,000 in the checking account. I did the math over again. Same outcome. I called the bank. I asked them where this money had come from. They replied, "Extra? It was there all along." There was $1,000 in my account I could not explain.

I think God was trying to make a point with me. Sometimes He doesn't repay you in money but He repays you in other ways. Maybe He leads you to a better job, a higher-paying job.

Tithing brings blessings. Giving is a way of emulating God's bounty to us. We are little children practicing how to be grown-ups, and God sees our efforts and rewards us as a loving parent will.

Calvary Revival Church was nondenominational but was influenced by the Assembly of God evangelical tradition. The church I now attend in Winchester is part of the Assembly of God denomination.

*   *   *

Terry had followed the path back to God along with me. God had been speaking to us both in His way.

Terry watched me get the children ready every Sunday to go to church.

Maybe after the fifth or sixth time, he started getting ready himself. I was just happy he was coming along. When we were ready, he was ready, and we all went to church as a family.

We've been going ever since. Terry is saved, and his relationship with the Lord is a deep one. We found our faith was not bound merely to Sundays, either. We began to have a daily family devotional that became a lifelong habit with us.

People go to church normally one day a week, maybe two times a week. In the meantime, our children are in the world every day. We seek to instill in them our values, but we also know these must be *their* beliefs come to by free will. But how do you choose when you don't even understand the choice before you? It's part of the process of maturing. A child should know *why* they believe what they believe.

For many years, we used a daily devotional called *Family Walk*.[1] Its strength was in its simplicity. There were three parts to each devotional: the story, the Bible reading, and then the application. We also ended our devotional time with a prayer.

We'd often do this in the morning. During our morning ritual hour as I'm combing their hair, one daughter would read the story, another would read the Bible verse that goes with it, and the third would read the application.

We bought each daughter her own Bible. That seemed rather revolutionary to me because I had never had my own Bible growing up. We had the big white Bible like everybody is supposed to have. It was on display, turned to Psalm 23 ("The Lord is my shepherd," and so on). A big Bible, collecting dust. But for the children to have their own Bibles—now that was something completely different from my own childhood experience.

We've heard the saying "God has no grandchildren." You have to know Him yourself. *Their* faith couldn't be *my* faith. They had to know why they believe what they believe. They have their own relationship with God. We can introduce our children to faith, we can help them along the way, but after that it is up to them.

I reflected that one obvious way to do this was to read the Bible myself, something I had neglected. So I sat down for the first of what would be many times, and read the Bible from Genesis to Revelation. I would reread it each year after that. I wanted to find out what it says. I didn't want to depend on other people to tell me what it contained, to tell me things that were possibly not true.

If I was going to live my life for the Lord, I believed I *had* to know what His words said. I couldn't go on somebody else's report. I needed to devote my time to know His word.

* * *

I liked those *Family Walk* devotionals very much. After the girls had grown up, I found myself still thinking in that structured manner about my own walk with the Lord—lesson, verse, application. But as an adult, the lessons that occurred to me were a bit more nitty-gritty, down-to-earth, and the applications more real-world adult. Once I read it closely, I found that the Bible was a nitty-gritty testament itself, full of applications to all of human life, including our latest modern variant. There is also, I admit, something of the Marine in the way I approach Christianity.

Eventually I developed a book, *Stop Being a Christian Wimp!*[2] This is a book that was out for a while but isn't available at present. I've currently pulled it to do a revision and develop a workbook to go along with the devotions.

Stop Being a Christian Wimp! was a God thing. It's devoted to down-to-earth topics in a thirty-one day devotional format. I made it a quick read because I wanted my readers to get to the Bible, to get to the verses I was pointing to, so they could hear directly from the Lord.

After the verses, I wrote a quick application that would lead to worship. One example: I tackled the topic of sleep. What does God have to do with sleep? A lot.

If you're worried about life, you're probably not sleeping properly. Try this: Get two pillowcases you can spare. Find a magic marker. Write the word "Good," on one pillowcase, "Evil" on the other. Now flip them over. Write "worry," "deceit," "trouble," and whatever else you can think of that's bothering you on the other side of the "Evil" pillowcase. On the other pillowcase, the "Good" one, write your hopes and ideals.

Now decide. On which pillow do you want to lay your head?

You're going to pick "Good."

It's a tangible reminder that we're supposed to rest, that God blesses rest. Plus it's a way to give ourselves a path to that rest.

It's practical advice. Trust God for twenty-one days, and maybe it will develop into a habit.

You may even think of it as a mini boot camp.

I felt the calling to write it. It came from the Lord. At the time, it seemed to me this was what the Lord wanted to talk about through me.

Eventually, I did seminars with the book, trying to give people hope. This was 2009, before I started my business. Writing the book helped me most of all. There are times when you learn a lesson all over again simply by teaching it.

* * *

There's a verse in Romans where Paul speaks of the gifts of God:

> We have different gifts, according to the grace given us. If a man's gift is prophesying, let him use it in proportion to his faith. If it is serving, let him serve; if it is teaching, let him teach; if it is encouraging, let him encourage; if it is contributing to the needs of others, let him give generously; if it is leadership, let him govern diligently; if it is showing mercy, let him do it cheerfully.[3]

It strikes me that these blessings are not limited because God is not limited. The gifts of God are allotted according to the individual, but they also apply to the stages of one's life.

When we give our lives to God, each of us is blessed on our whole life—on the gross, not the net. But to achieve that kind of blessing, we must be all in.

It had taken me years, but by my late twenties, I was all in. I have been ever since. I am not bashful about this fact. I try in every way to remove the filter between God and myself. And for people who don't believe me, who think I am faking it, all I can say is that I've got to care more about His opinion of the matter than theirs.

God has tested me with deep sorrow. He has also comforted me in ways even deeper, ways no human can comfort.

Gods asks us in the Book of Job:

> Where were you when I laid the earth's foundation?
> Tell me, if you understand.
> Who marked off its dimensions? Surely you know!
> Who stretched a measuring line across it?
> On what were its footings set,
> or who laid its cornerstone—
> while the morning stars sang together
> and all the angels shouted for joy?[4]

In Deuteronomy, He tells us He is beyond politics, possessions, and ideologies:

> Take heed unto yourselves, lest ye forget the covenant of the LORD your God, which he made with you, and make you a graven image, or the likeness of any thing, which the LORD thy God hath forbidden thee.
>
> For the LORD thy God is a consuming fire, even a jealous God.[5]

But in Hebrews the Lord promises "what cannot be shaken may remain." He says, "Since we are receiving a kingdom that cannot be shaken, let us be thankful, and so worship God acceptably with reverence and awe, for our 'God is a consuming fire.' "[6]

God is a consuming fire for me. When He speaks to me, He speaks to me. I will not deny this.

I certainly don't put politics above Him.

His call is easy to understand once you have heard it. "Whoever wants to be my disciple must deny themselves and take up their cross and follow me."[7]

He *is* in everything, and everything I am. I couldn't make it without Him. He died on the cross for me. If He will do that for me, there's nothing He won't do for me.

And for you.

Chapter Ten

THE STORM AND THE SHELTER

After my final semester at ODU, I had decided that I wasn't going to go to law school. My internship with the Norfolk Southern railroad had been contingent on my continuing my education. Since I had now graduated and was not going to go on to law school, the internship ended. I looked into getting a job at Norfolk Southern, but they didn't have any openings.

I applied to be a Vista volunteer. I was accepted and I did that for a while. At Vista, I instructed volunteers in how to teach adults reading skills and improve adult literacy. I found I wasn't doing the teaching so much as dealing with other volunteers and preparing reports to the board. But I was surrounded by the actual learning going on. It felt good to do good, to see adults getting an education, to see their lives turned around.

But the bills were coming due. We needed more money. I started looking for something else. One of the young ladies working with me in the Vista volunteers told me that there was a job opening at the Hampton Roads Chamber of Commerce (HRCC). I applied and they hired me. My title was program manager. HRCC is a regional five-city chamber comprised of the cities of Chesapeake, Norfolk, Portsmouth, Suffolk, and Virginia Beach. It was the regional chamber, and each division was located in a particular city, but the regional headquarters was in Norfolk.

At the Chamber of Commerce, I got to work with locally power-ful folks. Working for the chamber was political, as well. I remem-ber when I was first hired and learned that my job was to be mostly involved with education and educators. I told my boss I was a bit dis-appointed because I had wanted to be involved with politics. Educa-tion didn't have anything to do with politics.

Boy, was I young and naïve.

She told me in no uncertain terms, "Winsome, everything about education is political."

Of course I know that now, but I didn't realize it at the time. The Chamber was a learning ground for me in every way. I wrote speeches for my chairmen. I prepared documents. I met with business leaders. I was responsible for educational programs. Another program I man-aged was Leadership Hampton Roads, where we brought educators and business leaders together to mingle and exchange ideas. We taught principals of various schools how to be business-minded.

My job was to get the businesses to agree and facilitate the visit. Businesses were looking for employees with ability, and educators wanted to place their students. We brought them together. I ran a pro-gram called Partners in Education, and quite a few others. I worked at the Chamber for three years.

I enjoyed my time at the Chamber, but it was very demanding work. It was at the Chamber where I learned that you are only as good as your next event.

We put on such big events that we had to be extremely organized going in. We had to be disciplined. There were many deadlines for each of my programs.

I was responsible for initiating the graphics.

I had to secure the location.

Make catering arrangements if needed.

I had to organize the sign-in portion of these events, create name tags, manage the speakers and panels.

Me, as a toddler in
Jamaica.

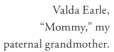

Valda Earle,
"Mommy," my
paternal grandmother.

Alberta Campbell, my maternal great-grandmother.

Sylvia Tucker, my mother's mother.

Olive Harris, my mother, at eighteen.

William Earle, my father.

Violet Earle ("Aunt Babs") and Gilbert Earle, my father's father.

Violet Earle Dexter ("Aunt Babs").

My grandmother's house. Unfortunately, this is my only photo.

The one-room house where Valda grew up.

Me visiting Kingston as an adult.

Me at eighteen, Stevenson senior photo.

Boot Camp Graduation, Parris Island. I am in the third row from the bottom, second from the left.

USMC PFC Sears
in the desert, 1983.

Second Lieutenant
Terence Sears,
USMC.

My husband and I when we were married.

Regent graduation. That's Rev. Pat Robertson presenting me with my diploma.

Janel and Katia outside our house in Larchmont.

Katia, Janel, and DeJon, 1993.

Janel in her Virginia
Children's Chorus
outfit.

Terry and I outside my Ninetieth District campaign headquarters, 2001.

Volunteers during my campaign for the House of Delegates, 2001.

My 2001 acceptance speech after winning the Ninetieth District seat in the House of Delegates.

Gubernatorial candidate and attorney general Mark Earley shakes my hand during our 2001 campaigns.

DeJon with Victoria and Faith.

Terry and me with
Victoria and Faith.

Me in the field with my M16, 1983.

Me after shooting an AR-15 during my 2021 campaign for lieutenant governor.

Glenn Youngkin, me, and Jason Miyares on the 2021 campaign trail.

On the 2021 campaign trail.

I had to figure out who might be in the audience that we needed to recognize.

It was logistics and much more.

Back then there was no GPS, so I would have to drive the route beforehand, plan the trip, and map it. Turn right here, turn left there in case you miss the bus. Rent the bus. All those logistics fell on my shoulders, and if it failed to come off, then I had failed. Everyone in the community would know. It was a very public position.

It was preparation for what I do now, that's for certain. My tasks required a constant attention to the details. I couldn't have my chairman show up at some event with him not knowing the who, what, when, where, and why of what was happening. I had to do the recon.

I was also responsible for several ongoing community committees, such as the veterans' committee. It was both a baptism by fire and also a wonderful place to work because you got involved in so many industries. You got to know a huge range of people, as well.

After three years, the Chamber began to downsize, and many more tasks fell on me. I was already overloaded. I decided it was time to resign and move on.

Soon after, I got a call from one of my old bosses. She asked if I would like to work for a Republican state senator from Chesapeake named Randy Forbes. I said sure. He's in politics; I've always wanted to be involved in politics. Forbes eventually became a congressman, but at that time he was a state senator. As I said, I wanted to work for the politician behind the scenes; that was the career I aimed for.

Randy Forbes is a lawyer, so I did mostly office work at first. I saw a curious thing at the Forbes law office. They are Christian folks, and one day Forbes's wife, Shirley, came in during my first months there.

"I need the tithe check," she said to our office manager.

I bided my time and asked her at an opportune moment. "Are you saying that *businesses* tithe?"

She said, "Yes, Winsome, some businesses do. We do."

I'll bet they tithed on the gross and not the net, too.

* * *

I wasn't at the Forbes office for long. Just when I thought I was starting to move forward with my goal, something happened that stopped
me cold for almost a year.

My old Marine Corps injury flared up.

As I said, I'd injured my back when the guys were playing a joke—
nothing nefarious—leaving me to try to lift a three-kilowatt generator,
which hurt my back. At the time, I heard a pop in my back. I was all
right at the time, but I knew that something had gone sideways inside.
Indeed, I'd hurt my back really badly. Like a tear that starts small but
slowly widens, it took a few years to reach its full effect. And the ripple
effects on my life and family lasted even longer.

It was bad. I couldn't walk for seven months.

I could not physically work. I put in a claim with the Marine Corps
for medical help, and they initially denied that I was hurt while in the
Marines. I appealed and won, and finally got the medical help that I
needed, but this took a few years.

I'm not sure what triggered the injury. I noticed that I was carrying
the baby on my hip and my hips seemed to go one way and the rest of
my back went the other way.

The pain went on and on. I ceased to be able to think straight
because I was in such constant pain. I couldn't walk. I couldn't even
crawl. I couldn't turn my neck. The nerve made every movement
excruciating.

The children and Terry had to do so much. My mother came up
several times from Jamaica and was able to help.

I prayed and prayed. "Lord, please don't let me be in this position.
I'm too young. Help me to walk again, Lord."

We found a chiropractor and he was adjusting my spine every week, applying electrodes and doing other work. Finally I could walk again. The Veterans Administration kicked in and we could pay for it.

This all lasted about a year. After about seven or eight months, I could sit up. My back healed. I could walk again.

Before this happened, Terry had taken a lower-paying job so that he could be home more with the family. We were soon in a financial mess. We were advised that we should declare bankruptcy to save our house, to keep it from foreclosure. This didn't make any sense, but they say a drowning man will clutch at straws, so we declared bankruptcy thinking that it would give us time. We hoped to reduce payments and save the house while we tried selling it.

But we lost the house anyway. The mortgage was foreclosed. We had to move.

Eventually, we paid everyone back. It wasn't the kind of bankruptcy that discharges all debts. This one got us lower payments, for all the good that did. By then I had found another job, and I was able to walk again. But we had lost the house, the first house we owned.

You know, when people say that I don't know what I'm talking about, that I've not experienced heartache and pain, they don't know. I started out as a single mother, then I had to care for three children under five while going to college and paying for college. I didn't have the GI Bill to pay for it. I had to pay for it on my own through financial aid and selling cars to bring money in. We bought a house and were doing all right until the old Marine Corps injury flared up.

But I'm the one whose father came here with $1.75. I was a U.S. Marine. You persevere, you do what you need to do. You don't quit, never give up.

It was gut check time, for sure.

* * *

After the house foreclosed, we moved elsewhere and rented in Norfolk.

I applied for a job at a company that did computer imaging. This was all very new. You could scan your documents—and they would be stored! Your information could be stored on this amazing device called a compact disc!

I was hired and we were recovering. I really liked the company and my coworkers, but I was uneasy. I did not feel this was the place I was supposed to be. At about five months working, I'd had a dream. I saw my boss surrounded by women and children, and they needed a home.

A month later, a job listing came through the fax machine. It said something about a homeless shelter. It turned out that my boss had been at the Salvation Army at their local board luncheon. During lunch, leadership happened to mention that they were looking for a director of their social services.

He said, "Winsome, I think you should take the job."

I said, "No, I'm not going. I like my job here!"

"At least go down and interview for it."

Actually, the job was not to manage a particular homeless shelter. It was for director of all the shelters, so the directors of the shelters would report to me.

As I was going down to the interview, I prayed, "I don't want to be stuck behind a desk. I would rather work with the women and the children, because then I would have a direct impact on their lives. I would be among them. I would be able to help them better."

Being the director of a single shelter paid much less, but I thought that would be a much more fulfilling position.

The interview went on for quite a while. I could tell my interviewer was interested and liked my job history. I never mentioned that what I wanted was something more hands-on, that I wanted the lower-paying job. Suddenly, my interviewer said, "You know, Winsome, I think we really would like for you to be one of the homeless shelter directors. I think you would just thrive in that position."

She perhaps thought I'd be disappointed or confused, but I smiled back at her and nodded yes.

Hope Center was located in Chesapeake, Virginia. It had previously been a colonial-style hotel before the Salvation Army turned it into a shelter. I believe originally the Salvation Army had used it as a residence for substance abusers before it became a women's residence.

I loved my job.[1] I could help people. Many were at rock bottom, and I could do something immediate and positive for them. I could really care for them in a practical way.

I'd seen my grandmother do it. She took in that homeless man and changed his life. She cared about the poor people in the community and looked after so many more. She would buy goods and distribute them to poorer neighbors: rice, sardines, canned meats, toothbrushes, and shoes.

I figured this would be my chance to help. I still had a lot to learn. It turns out that even being in a homeless shelter wasn't the bottom for some of the women. I would have to let them go, I would have to put them out because they created chaos for the other women who truly wanted to change their lives. Some went back to their old ways while they were in the shelter, including drinking, drugs, and stealing.

One lady in particular still troubles me. The police came to arrest her and I had to shield her children from seeing their mom taken in. I had to grab them and take them someplace else, and act as if nothing was happening. This was not uncommon, and we had to establish protocols. I'd call the next of kin or call child protective services during these instances because now the children were without a mother.

I would go to the jail and visit the arrested women sometimes when they ended up back there, because I did not want them to think that nobody cared. I wanted to let them know that when they got out they would have a home with us, that I would do everything I could to help.

Sometimes my staff said I was too lenient. This particularly happened toward the beginning of my tenure there, before they'd also seen I had a tough side. I gave our women *eight* opportunities to mess up. You can't throw people out at the first sign of trouble. These are women who often are doing their best at self-control, but have had terrible experiences to deal with. You have to give them opportunities to improve in increments. That's what we were there for, not to throw people out on the street again at the first infraction. You had to give them a second chance. Or a third. Or a fourth, fifth, sixth, seventh... and finally an eighth.

The shelter was divided into small apartments. Everyone got three square meals. We had a chef. I thought it would be good if the women helped, and we started that practice. This *wasn't* a hotel. Everyone had to put their hands to the plow. Even though we had a maintenance person, the yard needed to be swept. We taught them about independence, life skills, keeping house, finance, and education. So many didn't know how to do it all. They truly were never taught. What a small, but ongoing tragedy that creates in a woman's life.

We had a rotation of daily work chores. One week they were pulling kitchen duty, for instance, and so they would help the cook prepare the meals and clean up the facility. Another crew would help with the yard. One crew would help with the laundry. Idle hands make trouble! Each had to contribute both because we were family and because we were teaching life skills.

We did much more, too. One woman needed a whole mouth of teeth. We found a dentist who offered to do that, and I was the one who drove her to those appointments. I'd drive people to appointments, or one of the staff would. We had a social worker, too, at the facility.

It was a truly fulfilling time in my life.

The Hope Center had been through two or three directors in very short order just before I arrived, which meant that there was trouble there. I do thrive in ordering chaos. Normally when I come into a situation there's either a mess to deal with or an inefficient system in place, and I work to bring in a more stable, more workable solution.

My master's degree, which I'll tell you about shortly, is in organizational leadership, how to bring an organization into efficiency. So when I got to the center, I saw there was trouble and I got to work. There were times when the staff was against me, but things had to be done to set the ship right. Once they understood what I was doing—and I tried to involve them as much as I could—they realized I wasn't trying to make their lives difficult but was trying to make the residence a place where their own work would be effective. We couldn't survive in chaos.

After a time, we all came together, and it was wonderful. That's how it is for organizations. The new kid comes in and resistance follows. Then she's either accepted or somebody moves on.

Hope Center was a grand-looking facility. It sat on about six acres. There was the main building that housed the staff offices. It had laundry facilities, a dining room–style cafeteria, and the various hotel-style rooms with their own bathrooms. Up front we had an area that we called "triage." This was a place for new entries. Here we would keep a provisional resident under watch to see if she would be a good fit. In this area, we monitored them. The resident spent about six weeks there—with her children, if she had them—and if she did well, then we moved her into the main facility where there was more privacy and freedom. She'd get her own key. A true transition to independence.

We had women from all strata of society. We had single women, and we also had women who had children. We had women who were formerly incarcerated. We had women who had simply lost their jobs. We had women who were abused, and women who were running from abusive situations. We had women who had had everything and had lost everything. We had women who just needed a place to stay until they could get themselves back on their feet.

Instead of making those who'd broken the rules leave, I decided, Let's give them a measured amount of grace. That was when I put in place my eight opportunities to fail, or you could think of it as eight opportunities back to redemption. I could've made it ten, but I had to stop somewhere. It's got to be real. We were a Level 1 facility, basic, the next step from being back out there in society. If someone is causing chaos around herself and not advancing one iota in changing her life, we were not the facility for her. She would need a Level 2 or Level 3, with the kind of restrictions and enforcement we did not have or want to have in place.

My "strikes" might be the discipline of coming home at a certain time. The discipline of letting us know where you're going and being there when we check. The discipline of doing the chores when assigned. Your requirement to participate. The cleanliness of the common areas is necessary. The cleanliness of food, and food service, and food cleanup is necessary. There were no maids.

I saw it as an opportunity to help those who wanted help. It's the biblical concept of "whosoever will." Whoever wants help, we could help. But if a woman didn't want our help she could not stay with us. She would be interfering with the lives of those who did want to change. Enabling failure is not love.

*   *   *

During this time, my main job was being "Mom." DeJon, Katia, and Janel were the center of my home life. Terry and I took them to their activities: their plays, their choir practices. Janel proved to be a gifted singer who could hit high C. When we lived in Norfolk, she was part of the Virginia Children's Chorus. They put her at first soprano when she was six years old. I schlepped her here and schlepped her there, at least until she didn't want to do it anymore. I'm not a stage mom. If my kids didn't want to do it, fine.

Janel went on trips to sing in England and Wales when she was eleven. She's still a very good singer but she just doesn't use her talent as much as she used to. She has many other interests these days.

Katia was a singer as well. She also auditioned and was accepted into the Virginia Children's Chorus. I like to say they get it from me.

I'm a very prolific shower singer. But my husband is the real singer. He was an altar boy and a choir boy in the Catholic Church. When we dance, he'll sing to me. It's quite nice.

I said to my husband one time a few years after we married, "You know, I wouldn't have married *me* if I were you."

I had nothing to offer at the time. He had a degree. He was on his way in his career. I brought to the marriage a child. I was a single mom. I had not much going for me, to tell the truth.

I asked him, "So why did you marry me?"

Fine time for me to ask this question, right, with us knee-deep in children?

He said, "Because I saw ambition. I knew that one day you would do important things. And I love you."

Truly I could not have achieved what I have unless I had someone who was stable and who was secure within himself, someone who is not threatened by any success I have had.

Terry is himself indeed.

After I won the lieutenant governor's race, I was in a packed elevator, and one woman turned around and blurted out to him, "How do you walk in your wife's shadow?"

He plainly told her, "I *don't.*"

That's right. He doesn't walk in my shadow. He's his own man, his own person. *He* wanted me to run for lieutenant governor, that's how sure of himself he is. He told me I wouldn't be happy without going for it. I told him I was very happy.

He said, No, you should run.

We knew it was going to be a long, hard slog once again. At least by then we had a darn good idea of what we were getting into.

* * *

I was working at Hope Center for about two years when I felt the call to continue my education. I thought maybe I would try again for law school. I'd gotten in. Despite my yellow pad worksheet, I still had a lingering doubt. Had I made the wrong decision?

It was a dream, a fantasy, even, but it was wound up in pleasing my parents and grandparents, and so it was a hard one to let go of.

About that time we had a counselor at the shelter who was planning to administer a Myers-Briggs–style personality test to our populace. We had to figure out the how and when of administering the test to the women. The counselor said the best way to understand its uses was to take it myself.

That test put a lot of things in perspective for me. In answering the questions, I realized that what I wanted to do was change, to lead. Lawyers work within the system that they're given. You really must enjoy that aspect of the job, the jot and tittle of being a lawyer. Some people thrived in such a setting. I knew I never would. There was no use in trying to fit a square peg into a round hole.

That sealed the deal for me. I didn't want to be a lawyer after all.

Yes, I wanted something more. I just didn't know if I needed an advanced degree.

One year later I was accepted to Regent University into their public policy master's program in the School of Government.

I got to Regent by way of my forays into politics.

I had gone to a CPAC convention in 2000. CPAC, the Conservative Political Action Conference, is an ancient establishment in conservative politics. It's a huge convention for conservative activists, politicians, and those who work for political campaigns.

I had gotten involved in local politics in Norfolk already (more on that later). I figured that if I were going to be in government and politics then I should go for it and attend a CPAC.

When I got there I went to panels, heard speakers, and walked around looking at the display booths. Organizations buy booths and tables there, and put out their literature and all sorts of great tchotchkes. The Regent booth had rulers and water bottles and other swag. I took everything (as if I needed any of it!) and I felt so bad that I registered on the sign-up sheet.

Not long after, they called me. I said no, I don't want to come to Regent. I just wanted the swag at CPAC. Well, the next thing I knew, I got an application packet in the mail full of information about Regent. Still I was ambivalent. It was only a few months from when I had dusted off my acceptance letter to George Mason University and wondered if I should try law school again, decided definitely not to.

But the main obstacle, a true impediment, was that I had promised the Lord that I would pay all my debts after the bankruptcy. I had one remaining student debt—a student loan bill. I absolutely did not want to start a new educational venture before I had my debts paid off, and especially *that* debt.

Regent recruiting called me again. Finally, I went on a visit. I went explicitly to tell them that I was *not* coming, and to stop the recruiting efforts.

I visited and was impressed with the program. I told them I'd think about it. But I also said to them that I was going to need the Apostle Paul "knock me off my donkey" blinding sign that I could not miss.

As I was driving home, I thought about Saul (Paul) on the road to Damascus. I smiled. I'd set the bar impossibly high for the Lord.

Such things didn't normally happen to people. I was safe.

Just then, a voice spoke to me "Look up."

I looked up and there was a billboard. No one could miss this billboard. It was staring right at me on the highway as if it had been put up specifically for me. In giant letters it said, "Get Your Master's Degree at Regent University" and the copywriter had added in parentheses, "(Because you asked Him for a sign)." I laughed all the way home.

But I still had that outstanding student loan. Three weeks later

Regent called and asked if I'd made a decision. This time it was an admissions person, not recruiting.

I replied, "Yes, I believe I'm supposed to come, but I made a conflicting promise." I told the person on the phone about my vow to pay off the loan. He took this in stride and said, "We were actually prepared to offer you a full ride, Mrs. Sears."

Chapter Eleven

THE FIRST CAMPAIGN

Regent gave me the Mission Scholarship. With it comes the expectation that the recipient was to do something big in the world. I took that seriously.[1] But what would that be?

As you may know, Regent is a private Christian university in Virginia Beach, Virginia. Its motto is "Christian Leadership to Change the World."[2] At Regent, I was working on my master's degree in public policy. As usual, I liked my classes well enough, but there was something missing. Somehow, I wasn't in the right program.

I talked to one my professors. He said, "You know, Winsome, we have another professor and she's a prayer warrior. Maybe you should go in and pray with her and see how the Lord might be leading."

I visited her office. I told her my story and trepidations, then she got right to the point.

She asked me, "Why do you think the Lord was leading you to come here? Clearly He was."

I explained what was in my heart. She listened and then said, "Winsome, you're in the wrong place. You're supposed to be in *leadership*, not public policy. You're studying management when you should be studying how to lead."

She advised me to switch from the School of Government to the School of Leadership Studies, but with a government emphasis. Most of my previous courses were transferable.

* * *

So I was in the right place at last. As part of the servant leadership ideal at Regent, I'd become involved with the campaigns of local delegates to the General Assembly. I already knew several of them from my time working at the Hampton Roads Chamber of Commerce, but I had particular respect for Delegate Thelma Drake, who was running for reelection in the Eighty-Seventh District in the Virginia Assembly House of Delegates. Thelma eventually did become a U.S. congresswoman for the Second District in 2005.[3] At the moment, she was running for reelection as delegate.

I would accompany Thelma to events in the Black community, and I would occasionally write a speech for her, as well. I even wrote letters to the editor of the local newspapers.[4]

Thelma and I went to a meeting at one of the Black communities in Norfolk. It was a question-and-answer affair. Thelma took a seat up front and answered various questions from the audience. She talked about transportation, education, health care.

Suddenly the door flew open and in came another politician—a Democrat. He was White. He was not Thelma's opponent. He had been invited. They were both supposed to come and talk about whatever accomplishments and updates had happened at the General Assembly.

He was late. Because he was late, he and his entourage made a bunch of noise scraping the floors with the metal chairs, and this disrupted the meeting. He sat next to her and got many of the same questions Thelma had.

But something even more disturbing was to come.

People in the audience, which was mostly Black, immediately acted differently toward him. They became deferential.

Nobody owes a politician anything, least of all deference like that. Politicians are elected to serve. You answer to me, Mr. Politician, not I to you!

He was talking down to the audience, telling them that he was the only White man who had stood up for them in this matter or the other.

After a while, I'd had enough. I stood up and said, "How dare you come here and speak to us this way as if we are children, as if we can't dissect information!"

For a moment, he was confused. Why? Maybe because Black people are so often taken for granted.

I continued, "Thelma came and spoke about the issues that matter in ways that one would speak to *adults*. You speak to us as if we are your children. You would never speak to your White constituents this way."

He got red in the face and he started in on me. He called me a shill.

He was talking about what he'd done in the 1960s, not what he was doing in 2000. Black people were *right this moment* locked in a cycle of poverty. I asked him what he was prepared to do for us Black people *now*.

To my surprise, before he could answer, several of the people in attendance—people who were Black, jumped up and said, "We don't know her. She's not with us."

My heart sank. Didn't they realize that they owed him *nothing*? This is America. We don't worship our politicians. If you don't serve us, we vote you out! I was greatly troubled.

This was the moment when I decided all my inclinations, signs, and portents had been right. I *must* get into politics.

I wanted to "do a Moses." Let my people go!

The immediate upshot was that I decided I needed to take a year off from Regent in order to fully explore and accomplish this goal. After I explained my plan to my professors, I was able to arrange it without dropping from the program. But after my win, I lost my scholarship—or rather, I had to give it up to avoid mixing the college with political affairs.

*   *   *

I still had lingering thoughts of being a campaign manager, not a candidate. Thelma and others had spoken of a legendary political school put on by the Leadership Institute, practically a Republican institution.[5] The founder is Morton Blackwell, a national committeeman from Virginia.[6] He taught the ins and outs of the political industry. He taught every part of being a campaign manager: how to manage volunteers, get out the vote, create campaign themes, create literature, deal with the media, everything political. He's a stalwart in the industry.

So I signed up for a course there.

One afternoon about midweek we broke for the day. I went to take a nap by myself in my room. I was rooming with another person, but she was out at the time. Maybe I nodded off, or maybe I didn't. What did happen was that in that state of resting, I had a vision.

I saw a ring of fire. I saw it coming at me. I tried to get away from it, and it just kept coming toward me, like one of those rings of fire that the lions jump through.

I grew more and more fearful. I tried to run away from it but it wouldn't stop, wouldn't stop, until finally I had no choice but to turn and face it.

And as I turned and faced it, I had no choice but to step right into the ring of fire. I walked through it.

A voice spoke to me, "When you walk through the fire, you will not be burned; the flames will not set you ablaze. When you pass through the waters, I will be with you; and when you pass through the rivers, they will not sweep over you."

I awoke, or came out of the vision, and quickly pulled out my Bible. I found the words had been from the Book of Isaiah in the Old Testament, Isaiah 43:2, but the voice (or my memory) had reversed the order of the sentences.

Remember, by this time, I was well on my way on my Christian journey. I had found Calvary Revival Church and undergone discipleship training. I was reading my Bible; I was seeing the world as a follower of Christ first, last, and always.

In fact, I couldn't imagine what the Lord might want of me. But as it turns out, later that year the Hampton Road Republican delegates approached me about running for office.

Regent is a conservative, Christian-based school, and many of us students were active politically. Even though I had decided to take time off, I was still a student finishing up the previous semester's exams. I heard about a bus going up to the Republican Party's convention in Richmond. Mark Earley was attorney general, and he was running to be the Republican nominee for governor against Democrat Mark Warner, now Sen. Mark Warner. Earley was a Hampton Roads native. He was born and raised in Chesapeake. I knew Earley from my work at the Chamber of Commerce and had found him a humble, intelligent man who also was an excellent speaker.

At that time, he told me that his secret was to find out what the audience wanted to hear and try to be of service to *them*, not to some other agenda—advice I've long since taken to heart.

So I'd signed up for the bus and went to the Republican convention specifically to vote for Mark Earley's nomination. Unbeknownst to me, I wasn't on the roster to vote.

I felt there must be some reason the Lord wanted me to come all the way up to Richmond. I had exams to study for! I prayed about that, asked to find the reason I was there. Had it all been a waste of time?

The day passed, and we were soon to get back on the bus when I felt a tap on my shoulder. Someone beckoned me to follow. They led me to the Norfolk area delegation attending the GOP convention. They introduced themselves—I already knew many of them—and then they said to me, "We'd like you to run for office, Winsome. The Eighty-Ninth District."

At the time, the Eighty-Ninth was represented by the Speaker of the House of Delegates.

I told them I had to pray about it, and talk to my husband. I prayed all the way home on the bus: Is this why I came, Lord? Is this what you want?

I got home and Terry and I prayed over it. I decided to run.

But we were just coming out of our financial difficulties.

We had to find a house to rent in the Eighty-Ninth (since our rental had sold). One promising lead after another fell through. The only permanent lease we could find was a place in the Ninetieth District. That meant I couldn't run in the Eighty-Ninth.

I would have to put off my political activities.

That was when the Norfolk GOP called me and said, "Winsome, we'd rather you run in the Ninetieth."[7, 8]

I told them, you know a funny thing happened, and I happen to live in the Ninetieth *right now.*

* * *

I ran against Billy Robinson, an incumbent who'd held the seat since 1981. His father had served in the General Assembly eleven years before that.[9] The Ninetieth was majority Black. I had only three months to campaign against this Harvard-educated Black lawyer.[10]

Practically no one would fund me. I was running against a power-house.[11] It was brutal. Some members of the Black Muslims targeted me. I had to get a protective order taken out against the head of the local group.[12] I put my headquarters right in the Black community. He kept coming up to our campaign office door and threatening me and my volunteers. He was terrifying.[13]

I had to prove it to the judge and was granted my protective order. We got it. He was told to stay away from us. But he didn't.[14] He came up to me at a church when I was talking with some pastors. Billy Robinson was there, I told him this man had accosted me and called me the B-word. Robinson looked at me and said nothing. Then he got up, left the room, and walked away.

Eventually, the man was arrested. It was a circus. The group hired *my opponent* as their attorney! We were in a packed courtroom at the initial hearing, and here was my opponent questioning *me* on the witness stand.

He asked me the manner in which the defendant had violated the protective order. Well, how else could I answer?

"*You* yourself know," I said. "We were both in the church for the candidates' forum when I told you about it! You walked out of the room and you didn't say anything!"

He turned to the judge and asked him to please instruct me to answer the question as formatted.

The judge asked me to answer as instructed, but he was trying to hold back his laughter. The people in the courtroom were laughing under their breath. My opponent was losing his cool. Well, I'd been through hell and back, let me tell you, and when asked other questions, I made whatever answer I felt it necessary to make. Finally my opponent lost it and said, "Judge, will you please instruct the witness to not launch into soliloquies!"

Anyway, we eventually won the case.[15]

(Fast-forward twenty years later: I met the same gentleman again. He apologized and we moved on. Grace!)

I'd already been speaking about my financial troubles to various audiences during the campaign.[16] It wasn't a secret. It was out there. But someone on a state board of safety accessed my credit report and released all the details to local Black media.[17] This struck me as illegal, but I decided I didn't want another Black man to go to jail, so I let it be. But later while serving in the Assembly I saw his name come up as a nominee on that board list and had it struck.[18] Eventually, I filed a civil case against him. The lawyers negotiated and I received a settlement.[19] Twenty years later, I have yet to collect.

When I initially told my mother I was running, she said she was afraid they would kill me. Politics was not for the faint of heart. I told her I wasn't worried about that. This was America. They don't shoot politicians here. Perhaps I shouldn't have spoken so hastily.

My children were in public school. My youngest was ten years old. Other children would come up to them, no doubt prompted by their parents, and say things like "Tell your stupid mother to go back to Jamaica."

Why as Black people are we doing this to each other? And my God, why involve the children? If you don't want to vote for me, then don't vote for me. You don't have to destroy me and my family, for goodness' sake. And all this for a state-level political seat?

The slaves in the fields didn't die hoping their descendants would one day be beholden to a political party. No, they wanted their freedom. They wanted their families to be reunited. They wanted an education for their children. And now many Black people have chained themselves to the very party that wanted to keep their ancestors in slavery.

I had other death threats. It got bad. The state police wired my home and phone for tracing.

And of course there were the nude photographs! I'm not kidding. I was out knocking on doors, handing out campaign material, and talking about the issues, and people kept looking at me rather strangely. Finally at one door the lady there said, "Do you know what's going on? Have you seen the photos of you?" She pulled out a postcard mailer and there were indeed pictures of a man and woman naked, with my face Photoshopped on the woman's head!

On the front, the card said, "This is the Winsome Sears she wants you to see." It had some pious-looking photo of me. Then when you flipped it, it said, "This is the Winsome Sears she doesn't want you to know about." And there I supposedly was in these compromising positions with some man!

I do have to say I looked good.

They put my head on a fine-looking woman's body. Fabulous. I asked the person if I could have the card, and I took it and put it up in my campaign office!

It amused me for a while, but one of my volunteers said, "Winsome, that's just pornography, you've got to take it down."

"But I look great!"

"You've got to take it down."

So I did. Still have it somewhere. One of my souvenirs from hell.

Meanwhile, my volunteers and I were doing all the door knocking that we could. I had a lot of people working with me who had gotten tired of Robinson. They were tired of the nonsense.

They were hearing my message. Education. Personal responsibility. We are not victims, but victors. Black people are overcomers.

Enough people heard and agreed.[20] It wasn't a landslide. I won by only about six hundred votes.[21] But we won.[22]

I had no money to take a poll to know where we were. Then Billy Robinson finally agreed to a radio debate very late in the campaign. He came at me with such animosity, such vitriol, that it startled me. And then I realized it wasn't just anger I was hearing. It was fear.

Sure enough, the Democratic Party had taken a poll and realized that I was ahead.

That was when I finally started to get some funding.[23] Before then I was scrimping and scrounging, turning over the sofa looking for dimes, nickels, and quarters.

I did my own research on Billy Robinson.[24] He was an extremely successful criminal attorney known for getting clients off the hook.[25, 26] He'd also gotten a great many people released from prison,[27] and they would come back and terrify the neighborhood.[28] The people were tired of that.[29] It's exactly what's happening today. It was time for a change. That was my message.

Later, I led a men's prison ministry. So I want to help people return to society—but only if they become law-abiding citizens.

My campaign office was a storefront in a strip mall across the street from Booker T. Washington High School. I ran as a reform candidate. My message was hope, to be a politician answerable to the people. Servant leadership, just as I'd been studying at Regent.

My term started in 2002, and I served for 2002 and 2003.[30] I was the first Virginia Republican elected to a minority district since 1865, as well as the first Black female Republican elected to the House of Delegates, and the first immigrant woman. I was the first female veteran elected, as well.

I was conscious of the historical nature of my position. At the same time, I felt my accomplishment was not the point. I'd been elected to represent my district and I planned to do so. When I break such a historic barrier then, as now, I acknowledge its significance, but then get on with the job at hand.

Chapter Twelve

DELEGATE SEARS—I AM BLACK ENOUGH

The Virginia House of Delegates is awesome. The Virginia legislature is the oldest continuously serving legislative body in the entire New World.[1] It's been around since 1619. Again, I was the only Black Republican.

It was hell at first. I, perhaps foolishly, attempted to join the Black Caucus. I'm Black; they're Black. I figured I'm the only one who has a seat at the table because Republicans were in the majority at that point. We had a supermajority in the House of Delegates and a good amount in the Senate. *They* didn't have a seat at the majority table. I did. I said to them, why not let me help get the needs of our community?

I was very naïve about Democrat politics.

They didn't. Not a chance. They wouldn't hear of it. To which I say, God made me this color. God made me the best color for me. He made me Black.

Elsewhere things were better. I got my committee assignments. The committees were Privileges and Elections, Finance (which was almost unheard of for a rookie; it was one of the money committees), and Health and Welfare.[2]

I'd been to hell and back when I was elected. We freshman delegates chose seniority among us in a sort of raffle.

I thought, surely the Lord will reward me with the number one seniority. We came up for training—how to conduct ourselves during session, how to file bills, and all that. They put all the numbers in a bowl and we freshman delegates chose. I got third from last!

I was so angry with God. I questioned.

Lord, I suffered! This is my reward? Third from the last?

I was mad. The next day was Sunday. I promptly told the Lord I'm not *going* to church. I am mad that you did not give me a reward. Not going to church. The next day the whole family was getting ready for church. Maybe I should at least go...

I said to the Lord, "Okay, I'll go, but I'm just going to *sit* there, I'm not going to worship."

"I deserve I deserve" kept going around in my head. So we went to church. We started singing.

Okay, I'll sing. But I'm not going to *worship* because you were *not* honest with me!

Well, as you probably realized, when you start singing in church, you have already started worshipping.

And as I'm worshipping, the Lord gave me a vision. In the Marines you have a battalion. And in a battalion you have several companies. And each company is made up of platoons. There's a lot of people. I saw ranks of platoons, a great horde of companies, and as I lifted my eyes up, I saw the whole battalion. Coming down off a review stand is my commanding officer, Jesus.

He walks toward me. I'm out front. I'm standing at attention waiting for my promotion. It's very pomp and circumstance. Jesus turns, starts to pin me with my seniority, and I grab the award from His hands and throw it in His face!

And I gaze at Jesus and I see the hurt in His eyes. In my vision, He didn't say anything. He just looked sad.

Really, I deserve nothing, I thought. It's not about me; it's about Him and what He wants to accomplish.

I'd temporarily forgotten that. This was a very humbling experience.

Where is this servant leadership you've been talking about? I asked myself. When did it become about you?

Well, I just broke down. I said, "Lord, I'm sorry. I didn't realize what I was doing. Please forgive me."

*   *   *

The offices of all the Hampton Roads area delegates were placed mostly on one floor of the General Assembly building. It was named Seventh Heaven because we were all on the seventh floor. Hampton Roads is the general name for the group of cities down at the bottom of Virginia's enormous Chesapeake Bay. It's the second most populous area of the state. I had the old office of Delegate George Allen, who later became governor and then senator. My mentor Thelma Drake was next door. We were both from the Norfolk area. There were several others, including Bob McDonnell of Virginia Beach, who later became governor.

When I joined the General Assembly's Black Caucus they would have meetings before the meeting to which I was not invited. I was the only Black Republican in the legislature at the time (it would be another twenty years before another Black Republican, A. C. Cordoza, would be elected). After a while, this became an untenable situation because they were inextricably caught up in Democratic politics. I decided that I was *not* elected to be a member of the Black Caucus. I was elected to serve the people. I left.[3] It created a stir in the media, and I made sure to point out the hypocritical position that they held.[4] They should call themselves the Democrat Black Caucus and admit the group was entirely partisan.

During that minor blowup, I read where one caucus member said something that has become a litany over the years. It goes something like this: "We never knew how to fight her because she brings God into everything."

I guess in a way this is a backhanded compliment to my relationship with the Lord. It is true; I let Him fight my battles, and I listen for His voice. Instead of lashing out I refer it all to God. God will take care of things.

God loves my opponents, too, of course, and He's always there to guide them. It's not like I have a monopoly on acting according to God's will and being called according to His purpose! I might want vengeance against those who wish to use my beliefs against me, but He always has a way to bring people back into the path of grace. God created us all, and like a parent He tries to bring us to a place of redemption in the hopes we will ask for forgiveness.

I suppose the idea is that if my opponents can paint me as some sort of Holy Roller then they won't have to take my points seriously.

There is something in the idea that growing up in a third world country, one depends greatly on the spiritual side of life to get one through tough times. God can seem closest when we are most sorely beset with troubles.[5] But I came to my full faith in Jesus Christ in *America*. In *Virginia*, as a matter of fact.

* * *

In being assigned to the Privileges and Elections committee the then chairman, Lacey Putney,[6] who was the longest serving delegate in the House's history, said to me in an amazing western Virginia accent that sounded almost like Old English, "Delegate Sears, I would ha-uhve you to know-ah that this is the oldest commit-ay of the House, and it is also a ver-ah important commit-ay." I loved hearing him speak.

One of our first orders of business in Privileges and Elections was to hear the newly elected lieutenant governor, Tim Kaine, who was seeking to introduce legislation to fund programs he wanted to implement. Kaine, who is now one of Virginia's U.S. senators (and vice presidential candidate for Hillary Clinton), is a Democrat. Kaine needed to prove the necessity and funding source of his program. Having not overcome that hurdle, I motioned to dismiss his bill. My motion was seconded and we moved on.

*   *   *

During that first year in the Virginia General Assembly, I became directly involved in the Assembly's effort to deal with a national-level issue involving cross burning and the First Amendment.

Some KKK members had burned a cross on someone's property in Virginia Beach, a coastal city down in my neck of the woods. Bob McDonnell was the delegate from the specific district. The property belonged to an interracial couple, a Black man married to a White woman. The perpetrators of the cross burning were caught and convicted. The case was appealed to the Virginia Supreme Court, where the law was ruled unconstitutional.[7]

The problem was that the statute judged that defendants in a cross-burning case were guilty of intending to terrorize prima facie, and were doing it specifically by burning a cross. In other words, the law presumed them guilty by intent. The defendants had to prove they were innocent in intent. Well, we don't presume guilt in the American legal system, particularly if it is determining a matter of what somebody thought or didn't think in a general way about crosses and burning crosses. We need actual evidence of a defendant's mindset for most prosecutions. That's why there's a difference between first-degree murder and manslaughter, for instance.

With the statute thrown out, we were left with nothing in law, a condition I considered a great shame—and dangerous. The KKK might take it as carte blanche to go burning crosses once more—and get away with it on First Amendment grounds. We needed a new bill that would meet the Supreme Court's test for outlawing cross burning in most cases. We had to get around that problem of presuming intent.

And the problem was that a cross was a symbol—perhaps the world's most famous symbol—and to burn it was also a symbolic act—that is, an act of expression.

Virginia Attorney General Jerry Kilgore,[8] a lawyer from Scott County, was the only Republican who'd won statewide office in the 2001 election, despite the fact that we'd flipped the legislature. Mark Earley, my friend and sometime mentor from the Hampton Roads area, had lost to Mark Warner for governor, and Tim Kaine had won over Jay Katzen for lieutenant governor.

Anyway, Attorney General Kilgore wrote a bill and gave it to Delegate Bob McDonnell of Virginia Beach[9] to carry. The offense had happened in Bob's district, after all. I heard about it and thought that was an excellent idea. What's more, I, being a rookie, figured *two* bills on the matter would be better than one and would signal the legislature's deep intent to fix this problem. I didn't yet understand that once somebody had put a bill in, there was no need for another bill. All other comers were going to be combined in the same bill. Anyway, I went down to our bill writers and asked them to write for me a replacement bill for the old statute. It was essentially the same bill as Bob McDonnell's.

Bob saw me in the hall of Seventh Heaven one day in the Assembly Office Building. He was coming down the hallway and stopped up short.

He said to me, "Winsome, I'm going to let you carry the bill."

I was a bit befuddled. I said, "Thank you."

At the time, it didn't make any sense to me. Let me carry the bill? I soon realized that he could've easily had my bill folded into his. If he'd done that, I would've been just one of the patrons and he would be the chief patron of record. It would be *his* bill, with all the bragging rights that adhered thereto. I realized later he'd made a selfless, sacrificial political act. He could have used that bill as a feather in his cap to prove he cared about Black people, especially if he had plans to run for higher office. He would've been able to say, "I introduced the bill we passed to protect Black people from the KKK." It's a big deal because unfortunately the Democrats always accuse Republicans of not caring about Black people.

The fact that he would allow me, a rookie, to carry such a precious bill also indicated that he believed I had the ability to see it through.

It turned out there was a Democrat senator who sponsored a similar bill, but it was a very watered-down version. I didn't think that it would protect us from the forcible intimidation that cross burning produces. My bill passed in the House of Delegates and the Senate, as did hers, and the two bills went to a conference committee. This committee's task was to reconcile the two bills for eventual resubmission, passage, and a signature by the governor. That's how bills become laws.

The committee has three members of each legislative body and the bill sponsors. I argued for my version of the bill successfully. The Republican committee chairman, Sen. Ken Stolle, asked me if I were willing to take the burden on my shoulders that, should the law not meet the State Supreme Court test, we would then be left with no protection from the KKK.

The Democrats would make hay with such an outcome. Make me suffer.

Not to get into too many arcane details, but the bill had two sections. One was the old fifty-year-old Virginia statute prohibiting cross burning. The reason for keeping that in was that the law was about to be argued at the U.S. Supreme Court in Washington by the Commonwealth of Virginia. More on that in a moment.

The second section of the law modified the offending passage the Virginia State Supreme Court had struck down. So even if the U.S. Supreme Court ruled that the old statute was unconstitutional, then the new section would still apply.

The key to my bill was Section B, which says, "Any person who, with the intent of intimidating any person or group of persons, burns an object on a highway or other public place in a manner having a direct tendency to place another person in reasonable fear or apprehension of death or bodily injury is guilty of a Class 6 felony."

Notice the new wording. "Any object." This takes the burden from the fact that it's a cross specifically, with all the symbolism therein. Secondly, the new section also outlaws burning crosses or other material on public property with the intent of direct intimidation of individuals. This means, whether on public or private property, if there is an individual, say a Black person, whom the burning of a cross or any other object is directed against, a person who is meant to be directly intimidated by this act, then that burning becomes a crime. If it can be shown that the KKK fanatics are seeking to intimidate a particular person, they will be apprehended and prosecuted. By the way, the KKK hates Jews and Catholics as well. Crosses had been burned against them.

I said I was confident this section would pass the Virginia Supreme Court and even a national test. I felt strongly the need to uphold the attorney general and Bob McDonnell's trust in me to see this through. And the committee did adopt the stronger provisions of my bill. It passed 98–0 and became Virginia law.[10]

Before the conference committee, I went to the senator carrying the similar bill and asked her if she would let my bill go through, since I felt it was stronger. She was a Democrat, a Black woman. Her reply was very hostile, and a personal attack on me. I still can't understand where this hate for Black Republicans comes from. Why can't Black people just vote the way we want to vote? Why do we have to come and ask permission? Whose ring do Black people have to kiss? Who made those rules for us? Who says we're Black because we vote Democrat or not Black because we do not vote Democrat?

Atrocities were committed against Black people. There was slavery, prejudice, Jim Crow laws, and state-sponsored oppression. Yes, those things happened. But the world has changed and, while we will never be rid of people who are racist, surely we can admit that we are not back in those days? I mean Black people hold political office. We run companies. We take part in American society at all levels. Some on the American extreme left can't acknowledge progress because continually stirring the pot helps them keep anger alive for use toward political ends.

I ask you, what kind of a leader wants to keep the people seething against each other? That's so Machiavellian, so self-serving.

This is not the way things ought to be.

Several of the cross-burning statutes struck down as violations of the First Amendment had been appealed to the U.S. Supreme Court and bundled together into the case *Virginia v. Black*.[11] I was in the audience for the oral arguments on that case[12] not too many months later. The hearing was historically notable, of course, but also marked the first time that Justice Clarence Thomas had asked a question from the bench in years. He'd long made a point of desiring to listen to the cases of the lawyers on each side. But this was one time he made an exception.

Justice Thomas talked about how his grandfather growing up in the South had seen people lynched, had seen Black men lynched. He was asking a question, but it was a very moving moment of testimony that he gave. That same day, Justice Sandra Day O'Connor had asked questions that led those of us who had been conferring with the Virginia attorney general to realize that my bill was indeed safe.[13] That was pretty heady stuff for the kid from Jamaica.

* * *

I carried ten bills during my two-year term. I carried a bill to help us create more charter schools.[14] At the time we had five. My bill opened up the charter school process so that institutions of higher education could start related charter prep schools. An HBCU organization of historically Black colleges and universities asked me to carry that bill. They wanted education options for our children. People who say that charter schools are racist and instruments of White oppression might want to consider that HBCUs themselves wished to be involved in creating them.

My bill also gave charter schools the same immunity from prosecution as normal public schools. And it required reporting not only how many charters were granted, but also how many charter applications were denied and the reason for that denial. Twenty years later, Virginia only has nine charter schools.[15] The needle hasn't moved that much. In the meantime, North Carolina, our neighbor to the south, has 204.[16] Washington, DC, has 128.[17] As you know, Washington, DC, is a bastion of the Democratic Party, and yet they got it done because Black people wanted it and overcame teachers union opposition.

So why do Virginia Democrats keep denying charter schools when Black children have been failing spectacularly—yet when given the opportunity have flourished?

I'm not a Johnny-come-lately to the education process. It's something that I've been involved with for decades. When I ran for lieutenant governor primarily on education I could truthfully say: I know education. When I sat on the State Board of Education, I accepted no excuses. We need to understand why our children aren't learning. That's the primary purpose of school: to learn. That's why their parents are sending them to school. If schools are not going to do it because school boards take positions that destroy families and separate parents from their children, then parents need to be able to make a different decision.

We need school choice. We've needed it for some time. Choice in education will lift all boats. It will make the public schools better, and it will bring back the true purpose of education.

Unfortunately, it is still mostly a dream in the Commonwealth. But the day is coming when parents will make it a reality.

* * *

Partway through my term as delegate, I was reading in my local newspaper the *Virginian-Pilot* a story about how a doctor was killing patients through incompetence.[18, 19] The doctor was terminated at Hospital A. He moved on to Hospital B. Same surgeries, same deadly mistakes. It wasn't until he was at Hospital C that the medical board was finally apprised of his actions. The hospitals had been doing internal investigations, and this was a two-year process. In the meantime the doctor was out there killing patients via incompetence.

I said to myself, "Somebody ought to do something about this!" Then I paused and reflected that *I* was the somebody who should be doing it.

The article stated that there had been a JLARC commission report,[20] or a joint legislative audit review, of these medical practices, and this had found enormous problems. The report was three years old and had been gathering dust. Nobody wanted to touch it because it was so politically explosive. I decided that I was going to take it on. I called the reporter of the article and found out about the study. I called the chief architect of the study and we proceeded to start writing a bill for my second year. It would have to wait until the January session. In the meantime, I read in the papers that a delegate said I was committing political suicide by taking on the bill, and that I would not get any support for it.

I kept at it. When enough people saw that I was serious, the Medical Society of Virginia decided to work with me to help make it a good bill. I welcomed this. I'm not the expert; the doctors, nurses, pharmacists, and hospitals are. But something needed to be done, something needed to change to protect people from these glacial and disjointed investigations against medical malpractice. The people killed could have been my relatives; they could have been yours.

The bill, HB1441, was going to affect thirteen different state boards, so we had to coordinate with all of them. The study had found many egregious actions. Some doctors were signing blank prescription forms and leaving them for nurses to fill in. Those signed pads of blank prescriptions might get stolen or even sold. Funeral homes had issues, problems with bodies and chemicals. It was a huge tangle of problems. Many, many, many pages of a bill. We slogged through it all summer long.

We would meet monthly with the various lobbyists and representatives of all the boards. There was constant back-and-forth. But that's how you make good law. I wasn't the expert, but I was there to be sure changes would truly protect the public. That was the whole reason for creating the bill, after all. But we didn't want to hamstring the various medical professions unnecessarily.

After the third or fourth meeting, the Democrat commissioner of the Department of Health started coming to the meeting. Remember, the governor was a Democrat and I was a Republican carrying a massive bill. I thought this was great. Everybody was getting on board; the bill was getting favorable press. That meant everybody wanted in on it.

We put the bill in at the next session. Our attorney general (the same one whose cross-burning bill I carried) held a press conference because he would be one of the enforcers if it passed.

Governor Mark Warner during his State of the Commonwealth address that year talked all about the reforms to protect the public *he* was going to make at the medical board.

As we listened in the chamber, even the Democrats looked over at me as if to say, *We thought you were the one who was reforming the medical boards.*

Some of the newspapers who had been cheering us on turned on me. I came to discover that over in the Senate, the governor had a Democrat submit my bill as his own. I talked to our leadership and put a stop to that.

We had Republican State Senator Bill Bolling (who was to twice become lieutenant governor) submit my bill, and because Republicans controlled the Senate, we were able to fold the governor's bill into mine.

Politics. You've got to have the stomach for it, I guess.

The word "campaign" comes from war. You've got to have the stamina. Those who say that Christianity is a crutch ought to try using it as such in the political trenches. It's hard to keep a Christian attitude! The things that a Christian really wants to say, he can't. He has to remember that he's representing God. We are constantly asking for forgiveness because we are instructed to turn the other cheek! We often give in to anger and retaliation when we shouldn't.

The bill passed. The governor signed it, and it became the law.[21]

We did good. We helped protect people. That's what really matters. You have to take the punches when it's the right thing to do. That reform act was a massive undertaking. It had huge ramifications if I didn't get it right. There was the potential to anger so many powerful lobbyists and boards. Yet, as someone once told me, bills have sponsors, but laws don't have names on them. The only credit you get is the satisfaction of getting it done and the good it does for people.

My term was over at the end of 2003.

Everyone expected I would run again.

But I did not.

* * *

Terry had been offered a transfer to a job at the Virginia Inland Port. The Virginia port system is not just at the seacoast. We have a huge inland facility. There, things are done mostly by train. There is a hub in the mountains near Winchester, where the railroad goes through to points west. The new job would be a substantial promotion for my husband and bring in a good deal more money—but it would involve a move across the entire state of Virginia, literally a diagonal move of 215 miles from southeast to northwest. We resisted, but they kept sweetening the pot more and more. Terry was outstanding at his job. They really wanted him in that position.

More important and ominous, my oldest daughter, DeJon, began to develop problems. Little did I know it, but this was only the beginning of grueling years of her troubles.

DeJon had gone away to college. While there, she had a total breakdown. It was so bad, I had to go and get her.

The problem turned out to be far worse than anything I could have imagined. This was no collapse from college stress. I had to retrieve her from the psych ward at a local hospital. She'd had a psychotic break.

DeJon was diagnosed as clinically bipolar.

We didn't know until then. There were times that she'd behaved strangely. She was a teenager; we thought that she was just being rebellious. We didn't know the signs. Now she was going to require a great deal of care.

And yet politics still called to me. I was asked to run for U.S. Congress against Democrat Bobby Scott in the Third Congressional District.

Chapter Thirteen

MY ONLY OPPONENT
IS ME

Running for U.S. Congress was *not* my idea. I said no at first. I told them I was done with politics and my daughters needed me. But then I was confronted with the votes that my eventual opponent had taken over the years. One that stood out was Bobby Scott's vote against the Child Custody Protection Act.[1] The law would have prohibited an individual from taking somebody else's underage daughter across state lines to get an abortion. It could be your daughter. It could be mine. Such a person could then just drop her back home as if nothing had happened. And of course we know that a lot of underage girls are sexually trafficked by much older men. They're not prosecuted if they take a girl in for an abortion.

Furthermore, he had voted against a law banning possession of computer-simulated child pornography,[2] claiming possessing such filth was a First Amendment right. He actually fought *against* that bill in the U.S. Congress. This type of porn is so real in appearance that they couldn't even show it on television. He fought for that at the ACLU's urging.[3] He felt so safe in his seat that he was one of eight "no" votes in the U.S. House of Representatives (all but one of which were by Democrats).[4]

The local newspapers reported this, but when I brought it up during my campaign, they acted as if it had never happened, that I was making it up. They refused to verify my point. I learned another lesson then.

I was coming up against another political giant, our first Black congressman since Reconstruction. But everything he stood for and, more important, voted for was hurting our community.

Abortion is a scourge for Black people, a eugenics project run against the Black family. Bobby Scott has to this day, eighteen years later, a National Abortion Rights Action League score of 100 percent.[5] This means he has been given an A-plus by the biggest abortion lobby in the world. A perfect record. Appalling on his part. Black women make up about 6.2 percent of the Virginia population[6] but have 41 percent of the abortions.[7]

The Third is a majority Black district. Ultraleft Democrats had their man in place. Republicans had had no luck trying to unseat him. They'd been shellacked in election after election.

If not me, who stood a chance? No one.

I prayed and prayed about it. I talked to my husband. He wasn't in agreement on this one. He wanted the move, the new life with me and the girls, the new start. But he has always figured that once the Lord spoke, we would follow His path.

I'd been running away. I knew what I was supposed to do. But how many giants can you face? How many lions can you stand down? How many times do you have to engage in such a public life?

I knew that this was what the Lord wanted because I knew it was the right thing to do to oppose this barbarity. So I said goodbye to the family and moved back to the area.

I brought DeJon to live with me, and she accompanied me on the campaign. This was necessary because she had been prescribed medication that she had to take, and take on schedule. The doctors were clear about this. Because of the nature of the disease, the person swings through a period of comparative normalcy. They will often feel fine and stop taking their medication. A crash inevitably follows.

I have to admit that despite her breakdown, I thought DeJon would get better, to the point of going back to being the old DeJon.

I was underestimating the disease.

But she did *seem* to get better. I had hoped the medication had been adjusted correctly and was working. I didn't begin to comprehend the malignancy of the mental illness that had overtaken her. Not then. Not yet.

This time I didn't live across the water, as we say. I wasn't in Norfolk anymore. I needed to be on the peninsula. When you considered the Third District as it was then configured, it looked like a salamander. It had a boundary that went more or less straight up from Norfolk, curved across the water and continued in a winding manner to Richmond to pick up some Black population there.

It was a carved-out Black seat, two and a half hours from point to point.

It had been created to ensure that Black Virginians had representation.

After I was asked to run, nobody would give me money. It was the same old same old.

I encountered the Democrats' political machine in the Black community head-on. I'd meet church members who were deeply concerned about the effects of these terrible choices our culture and institutions had made.

Abortion is a plague on Black people. There's much I could say here, but suffice to say that if we Black people don't vote differently, we will continue to have the same problems.

Suffice to say, it was a very difficult campaign, but then my other run for office had been hell on wheels, so why should this one be easy? But, then, my whole life hadn't been easy.

We gave Bobby Scott the hardest run he'd had in years. We made a difference in that district. If we couldn't deliver hope, we planted the seeds of hope that things might change, that the years of dependency and kowtowing to a political establishment didn't have to continue.

That treating its constituents like so many head of cattle in the pasture might end.

I lost the election. Well, the world would say I had lost. But I again think of it in biblical terms. Didn't God send prophets? Weren't some of them reviled? Weren't some of them killed? Yes. Would you say that they lost? Man looks at the end of a mission to judge whether you are outwardly successful or not.

God just wants to know, "Did you obey Me? Did you do what I asked you to do?"

You are successful the minute you set your mind to obey. It doesn't matter the outcome. So I say I won that race. Here's what I believe about competition in all its forms: I am my only real opponent in everything. I am the one who can keep myself from doing what the Lord requires. I am also the victor when I do His will.

Chapter Fourteen

THE LORD GIVETH, THE LORD TAKETH AWAY

After the 2004 congressional election, I returned to Winchester with my family. We discovered something.

DeJon was pregnant.

She'd gotten pregnant at college. Of course, I blamed myself for missing this. My blame did no good. She was pregnant and she needed help dealing with it. Her disease caused her to engage in activity out of character for her.

The disease was fierce, something beyond all my experience to that point. As the doctors told us, the sufferer feels extreme highs and extreme lows. Normal behavior, normal ways of thinking, disappear during these times. With medication, relative normalcy returns, and the person seems to be all right. Then they will often stop taking their medication and immediately revert to the highs and lows. They don't sleep during the bad swings. When they are on the high portion, they take risks, often crazy risks. We were only just beginning to understand what this meant for DeJon.

DeJon was an adult. We couldn't force her to stay at home with us. Even when she did, we had a hard time keeping her on her medication. Even though her mental illness had not abated, DeJon had a normal pregnancy and delivered a beautiful baby girl.

Her name was Victoria. By mutual agreement, Victoria came to live with us in Winchester.

Katia and Janel were still in high school. I found myself raising an infant once again. As if in some manner recapitulating my childhood, sometimes Victoria stayed with us, and sometimes with her mother. At times DeJon would be doing fine, taking her meds, and then other times she would just be gone, physically gone. We wouldn't know where she was.

One time we got a call from the sheriff that she was in jail because she'd had a psychotic break again. They couldn't find a local hospital that could take her; there were no beds to put her in.

Twenty years later, the Commonwealth still has this issue. We do not take care of mental illness as we should. Many of the social ills we see around us such as homelessness and street dependency can be traced directly to our failure to adequately treat the mentally ill. People who have mental issues end up in the jails. And if they don't have family with the means and the will to get them placed elsewhere, they often stay there and get worse and worse. Even more terrible, they are outside with no supervision or help. Each one is often a tragedy unfolding in real time.

We had to have DeJon committed several times. Finally the doctor said we would just have to watch her physically take her medicine every time she took it. We tried, but she was an adult. We had no means of coercion.

She was truly like two different people when she was on her medication and when she was off it. On it, she was the DeJon we knew. When she was not taking her medication she was a totally different *personality*. I mean, we didn't know her. She would take it, then get off for extended periods.

And she got pregnant again.

We tried to help. We would watch her take her medication. We would make her stick her tongue out so we could be sure she'd swallowed it.

For a while, she was doing well. She'd gotten a job and moved into her own place. Her second baby was born and lived mostly with us.

DeJon named her Faith.

Terry and I raised Victoria, and then Faith, for nearly seven years. They often stayed over with their mother, but they lived with us. Terry and I were the ones raising Victoria and Faith. Our other daughters had by now gone off to college. We fed our granddaughters. We bathed them. Got them up in the mornings. I took them to daycare. We had family devotions as we did when their mother was younger and their aunts were little.

People have sometimes speculated about what I was doing during the time I was out of politics. Well, there it was.

I was deeply involved with parenting infants, toddlers, and then young children once again.

My grandkids were a deep blessing. Even now, it's almost impossible for me to write about this, mostly because I cannot convey the joy they gave us even as we sorrowed for the suffering of their mother. Suffice it to say that Victoria and Faith were a blessing!

Once DeJon seemed permanently stable, I wanted them to stay mostly with their mother. I wanted her to be a mother, and DeJon wished to try this, as well. I didn't want to come between her and her own children. So they went to live with their mother in early 2011. All seemed good.

Then I began to see signs that things were not well with DeJon. Again, the disease fooled her and made her think she was fine, she didn't need to stay on the medication.

One day she was bending over to pick up Faith. Faith was five by then. She bent down to get her, and as she did DeJon turned her head and looked at me.

I did not see Dejon's face. I saw a skull looking at me. I saw it as a vision. Her face had become a skull. Then the vision went away.

My first thought was, Oh my God, DeJon has stopped taking her medicine again.

I couldn't get her doctors to give me any information. She was an adult and they couldn't tell me what was going on unless she approved. I wanted to keep the peace. Once again, I didn't really understand how bad it was. We had so recently seemed to have our DeJon back.

Yet the truth was the disease had progressed. There was no cure, and no going back. Afterward, I saw that her home was a mess. You could see the chaos in her mind reflected in her apartment. One of the doctors early on had said to me that she would not be able to handle very many of these psychotic breaks. Each time she experienced one it was destroying her brain.

You ask yourself, What could I have done? What could I have done? I just did not comprehend how bad it was.

We still kept the kids often. There is nothing grandparents love more than babysitting. We gloried in it.

A month before what happened came about, Faith, who was only five years old, started talking about one thing over and over.

"Grandma, Jesus is going to give us a big house."

"What? What house?" I asked.

"A big house!"

Faith would continue talking about her big house from Jesus, and she even started drawing big houses with markers and crayons. Pictures and stories. One evening when I was putting her to bed, she looked up at the ceiling, closed her eyes, and said, "Thank you, Jesus, for that big house you're going to give us."

After Faith had gone to bed and DeJon had come home, I asked, "Are you moving?"

"No. Why?" DeJon asked, puzzlement on her face. We shrugged it off.

One day the grandkids were over, and we had a full house. DeJon was in the kitchen with my husband. My daughter Janel was home from New York. She was sitting on the couch with Victoria on one side of her and Faith on the other. I was opposite them in another chair when Faith skipped over, sat on my leg, and gently leaned into my side.

"Can I ask you a question, Grandma?"

"Of course," I replied. But I never heard the question.

I still to this day don't know what to call it. But I'll call it a "voice." The voice filled the entire room and asked, "What are you going to do if she dies?"

I looked across at my daughter Janel to see whether she had heard the voice, too. But everyone continued doing what they were doing. Then Faith jumped off my leg and stood in front of me. I studied her face, the curvature of her nose and mouth. I memorized every detail, the tiny dent in her upper lip. The lashes darting out near her bright eyes.

"Grandma!?" she shouted.

Huh? I realized I had been on a different plane.

The next day, DeJon experienced her final psychotic episode.

She put the children in her Honda Civic and started driving down Lee Highway in Fairfax, Virginia, at a terrific rate of speed. Somehow DeJon sideswiped another vehicle, hit a median strip, then T-boned into another vehicle.

Around the proverbial three a.m., two sheriff's deputies knocked on our door. Terry answered, and I walked up. I heard one say, "DeJon is dead. Faith is dead. Victoria is on life support."

My knees buckled, and I collapsed into a chair. Janel screamed. My husband was simply hushed.

One thing started running through my mind over and over.

The Lord giveth, and the Lord taketh away. Blessed be the name of the Lord.

That's from Job. Job lost his children, too.

And then I said it out loud, "The Lord giveth and the Lord taketh away. Blessed be the name of the Lord."

"You have so much faith," the deputy answered. "I'm so sorry."

I had faith in the Lord. I have faith in the Lord. However, the Lord decided I wouldn't have DeJon or Faith or, the next day, Victoria, either.[1] Victoria had no brain waves. We took her off life support and donated her organs.

We have had family get-togethers with one of the organ recipients but not the other. He never thanked my granddaughter for saving his life.

*   *   *

Sudden accidental death is a shock to your system. For a while, I was literally collapsing from the grief. I would just find myself on the floor. But my faith in God made the difference. I couldn't have survived without Him.

The month before the accident, DeJon hadn't understood the messages that were being sent, and neither had I. After a ton of pain and grieving, I got it. Faith had been looking for the word "mansion," though she was too young to know it.

The hurt wasn't quite as hurtful anymore because our Lord had let me know that he was going to take them home. Home. That's where we all want to be.

My mother said to me, "When you had the vision and when you heard the voice about the children and you saw the skull in her face, you should think as a mom if the Lord had wanted you to take DeJon's car keys, if the Lord had wanted you to keep the children with you, if the Lord wanted you to get her in a hospital, He would have made you know that you should do those things."

She went on to explain that He would *know* that I was missing the signs. He was God, after all.

But that wasn't the purpose of what He'd shown me. It was to let me know that He was going to take them home. It was to prepare me.

The relationship that I have with Him is such that He knew that I would've probably walked away from Him. I would say to God, You were going to take my child and my grandchildren and You never said anything, You never warned me. You tell me everything else, but You didn't even do that. There is no love in that.

So I was satisfied. He did send me a sign to prepare my heart. He showed me that His hand is in all things, even in that. As it says in 2 Corinthians 5:1, "For we know that if the earthly tent we live in is destroyed, we have a building from God, an eternal house in heaven, not built by human hands." My five-year-old granddaughter was excited to be going to her big house—her mansion.

* * *

Second Corinthians 4:8–9 says, "We are hard pressed on every side, but not crushed; perplexed, but not in despair; persecuted, but not abandoned; struck down, but not destroyed."[2] The world is so often trying to tear us down. But we have hope. "You prepare a table before me in the presence of my enemies," says Psalm 23. "You anoint my head with oil; my cup overflows."[3]

People may say that doesn't work for everybody. There's poverty, disease, and war. All kinds of trouble. But the real enemy is a spiritual enemy. The ultimate enemy is Satan. When I die, I go to heaven no matter how I die, whether I die as a baby in the womb, or as a result of a car accident when I'm older, or even if I die quietly in my bed at ninety-five years old. I'm going to die no matter what—and when I do, my enemy cannot defeat me and drag me away. I go safely to heaven. This world was created perfect. Now, there is chaos.

It's only when you're in a crisis, in a critical time, that the words of the Bible really become true to you. That's what you're hanging on. What did He promise? What did He say?

I thought I knew all that the Bible said about heaven, but it's only when you need it that you remember it, or you go truly seek it. Now that they were gone on to heaven I wanted to know: What is it really like? What are they seeing?

Information about heaven is in Genesis and throughout the Bible all the way to Revelation. In Genesis, we learn that heaven has angels, servants, and messengers of the Lord.[4] In Revelation we learn that there is no sun: "The city does not need the sun or the moon to shine on it, for the glory of God gives it light, and the Lamb is its lamp. The nations will walk by its light, and the kings of the earth will bring their splendor into it. On no day will its gates ever be shut, for there will be no night there."[5]

God and Jesus, the Lamb, provide the light. I try to imagine that much light emanating from God. We learn that there really are pearly gates. There is one big pearl that opens each of the gates. The Apostle Peter isn't there opening them up, at least not in Revelation, but each gate is one giant pearl: "The twelve gates were twelve pearls, each gate made of a single pearl. The great street of the city was of gold, as pure as transparent glass."[6]

In Revelation, we learn about the throne of God.[7] God *and* the Lamb are on the throne.[8] In Isaiah, we're told of the train of the Lord's robe filling the temple in heaven,[9] and how the place shakes from the voices of angels singing.[10] All throughout the Bible we find images and details of heaven sprinkled hither and thither. You learn about the cherubim and the seraphim; I always wondered what the difference was, until I read in Ezekiel where he says that the cherubim have the face of an angel, a man, a lion, and an eagle.[11] And we learn of the appearance of the seraphim, and their wings, in Isaiah.[12]

My children are seeing these things. They're looking at the throne.

A crisis will bring you to what you really believe.

I questioned. I thought of Psalm 121:7 where God says He will protect us from harm. I went back to the Scripture and saw that's not exactly what it says. When you look at the Hebrew, especially, it says He will preserve your *spirit*, your soul, from harm. In Jude, Archangel Michael fights with the devil for the body of Moses.[13]

The devil is full of hate, he's full of anger, he's a destroyer, he's a liar, he's everything that God is not. But he is not the opposite of God. Satan is a created being, an archangel. He was made by God. He rebelled, yes. When the devil came after Job, the devil didn't create the weather, the wind, and the water.[14] He just twisted what was already there. He has great power in the world, but he has limits. God has no limits. God preserves the soul.

Chapter Fifteen

THE GO-GO YEARS

I stayed away from politics. I had come off the grueling campaign for Congress in the Newport News–Richmond area. This was four and a half hours away from Winchester. I moved back up with my family, and it seemed far, far away from all that.

Anyway, until we were able to get our house, we lived in a condo. For two years I hadn't seen items that we had packed and put in storage because we just didn't have the room for them. I thought to myself, If you made it fine without all these dishes and the furniture and knickknacks, maybe you don't need them. They were gone for two years, after all, and you didn't miss them.

But it was like Christmas going into the storage unit and putting everything into the new house. Oh—we own *this*! Oh—we have one of *those*! I forgot!

* * *

In Winchester, I took a job as the CEO of the local Realtor® board, the Blue Ridge Association of Realtors. Our association had about eight hundred members. It's a small town, a less populated area in the Northern Shenandoah Valley. It was the go-go days of buying and selling homes, of flipping them for profit. All over America, people were going wild with the technique. It was off the charts. There were no down payment loans, and it seemed like the market would keep going up and up and up.

People were building McMansions. You'd buy a house one day; you'd turn around and sell it the next. There didn't seem to be any questions. Everything was fine—fine, that is, until the bottom fell out, until the subprime loans came due. Another thing was that the Wall Street folks had junk mortgages and would bundle them so you couldn't tell one good mortgage from another bad one.

Furthermore, people were calling these mortgages "liar loans," since no one really checked whether the applicants were truthful. Everything went wild. Many people were caught with homes where the interest rate skyrocketed on a variable interest loan and they just couldn't pay. They simply could not make their mortgages.

So the money became dangerously easy to borrow, and boy, was it flowing. All the while, the mortgage bankers were repackaging them in bundles where investors couldn't tell the good from the junk mortgages. People were speculating on those like they were stocks. It was crazy, and nobody was asking the basic question: Can the borrowers really afford these houses?

The whole edifice came crashing down. People literally lost everything. I remember in my neighborhood there was a police officer who owned five houses worth $500,000 each, and he was paying for them on a policeman's salary. That was how crazy it got, and people were flipping, flipping, flipping, until somebody got caught holding the bag. Even people who knew better got involved.

My husband and I got caught ourselves to some extent because when we first moved we rented a condo while waiting for prices to stabilize, and after two years we were ready to get out of there. Prices kept going up and up so we figured we had to jump in—otherwise we wouldn't be able to afford it. So we bought our house, but unfortunately we jumped in at the very top of the market with a variable interest rate mortgage.

Thank God we managed to hang on; we're still here. We didn't lose our house.

When the bust came, houses were being abandoned left and right. They stopped building our subdivision partway through. Houses were selling at less than half of their former value. I hope people remember how bad it was. Those who lost their homes—they remember. And those of us who made it through by the skin of our teeth, we remember, too. We may be seeing similar conditions now, but things never play out in exactly the same way. Who knows?

The government tried to provide remedies on the adjustable rate mortgage debacle, and they came up with crazy rules that often made the situation worse. They forced people to take stupid measures, to behave in a way that makes no sense to anybody, such as to let their mortgages go into default in order to obtain a fixed rate loan.

The sort of thing is what would happen with the government bailing out student loans. It won't benefit the poor. In fact, it hurts the worker in trades, the plumbers and electricians and welders. They don't have these loans. They work and pay taxes. It benefits those who don't need it. People who went to college took these loans and understood when they took them that this is what they promised to pay back. It makes no economic sense. It's morally wrong. They're not saving everybody, as they claim. They're bankrupting us. This is what happens when you have government involved in banking on an individual level, calling winners and losers.

* * *

After working with the real estate association for a few years, I started praying about starting my own business. It was time to try something new.

I guess I should've asked the Lord for maybe a bridal salon, but what I ended up with was an appliance repair, plumbing, and electric company.

I bought the business from someone at church, but what I bought was just the name and phone number. There were no employees, no trucks, no tools, no office furniture, or location to put it in.

The real estate recession was upon us. People were losing jobs left and right. Some had lost their savings. Nobody was hiring. People were renting rooms in their houses to make ends meet. In some places, it was almost like the 1930s again. Here I was with a business I had to rebuild from the bottom up.

First I joined leads clubs, bought mailing lists, and went online. I sent mailers, and knocked on doors and dropped off my business cards, phoned customers. I found my first subcontractor. That was how we started.

What does it sound like? A political campaign!

The Lord was leading me back. As I was building this business from scratch, I kept being reminded of how like campaigning it was. You're starting a whole new organization; you're building an organization from the ground up. You work it and you work it. "Hi, my name is Winsome, I want to introduce my business—" Many people hang up at that point. You keep at it. People don't need your services, people can't afford your services, people want to know how long you've been in business. What could I tell them on that one? A week. *And I'm supposed to pay you my hard-earned money? Yeah, right.*

* * *

Shenandoah Appliance, Plumbing, and Electric was a home repair company. We did everything by house call. After a while, I made deals to subcontract with home warranty companies. This brought in a lot of business, because when an appliance such as a refrigerator or dishwasher broke, they'd call their warranty company and the warranty company would send us out to fix the problem. But I found out that some home warranty companies are extremely shady and untrustworthy. They wouldn't pay, they wouldn't honor repairs and would leave us to collect the bill. I went as far as reporting one such company to the attorney general of New Jersey. It took a while to figure out who you could trust, who was on the up-and-up and who were the scam artists. We also had a few customers who were out to get service without paying, or claim damages our guys had nothing to do with, and have us pay for their repairs. We learned to mark preexisting damage and record it with photos to protect ourselves.

But for the most part, our customers were great, and we strove to give them the best service possible. This is how even the inconveniences of life can bring blessings with them. Many of our customers simply wanted prayer! Imagine that! So either I or our repairman would pray for them.

We learned. We added trucks and employees, then health care and vacations. We eventually did very well. Both of my daughters got involved in the business. Some weeks at the beginning I didn't know how I was going to pay my employees, but the Lord came through and I'd get a customer, then another customer, and we'd finish the week strong.

We added more trucks and employees. The employees were in and out of our house, phones were ringing, faxes buzzing, parts deliveries coming in, paperwork taking up our formal dining room—our HOA was not too happy with the situation! Finally my husband said, "That's it! You have to get out of here! I want our house back!" So we moved out of the house and got our office space. We did very well for more than a decade. We started in 2010. We grew and grew.

The thing that killed us was the government's botched response to the Covid pandemic. Home visits became a nightmare to deal with, and then impossible. Afterward, we simply couldn't rehire any employees. People had either moved on or were living on subsidies from the government. We couldn't hire. We had cannibalized employees until one company could pay better.

I believe that the business was designed to bring me back into politics. I had to learn to say no to customers who wanted to jump the line, no to customers who berated and threatened to report me to every single authority there was because they didn't get their way.

I had to fight for those customers who had home warranties with the very companies who refused to do the right thing and honor them. I advocated on these customers' behalf. I had to sometimes fight government itself on issues that didn't help businesses.

In fact, there was one state I wanted to expand into, but they made it so onerous to start a business there I withdrew from the attempt. It took two years for us to try again, and only when it appeared there was significant customer base there to justify the effort to cut through the red tape. I learned how to serve graciously. I found that sometimes customers just want to hear from someone who cares. At times we went above and beyond just to make a customer feel that someone cared. We did it because it was the right thing to do, even if they sometimes couldn't pay. We would help a person who was desperately in need, believing God would bless us in some other way. Sometimes all a customer wanted was prayer. They wanted someone to come see about them. They were often elderly and lonely.

By that time, my daughters had found other things to do, as had I—such as running to become lieutenant governor of Virginia. Shenandoah Appliance, Plumbing, and Electric is no more.

DeJon and my grandchildren went to heaven in 2012.

I had been appointed to the Virginia Board of Education by Gov. Bob McDonnell in 2010. The time had come for me to consider a return to elected politics. The only question was: Was the Lord leading me to do so—and, if so, what did He want me to do?

Chapter Sixteen

SENSE AND SENSIBILITY

We have to know what's going on in our schools. We have to know that our children are learning. We can't set the test standards so low that the children don't learn anything. They've passed, but we've made the bar so low anybody can pass. You're going to need a good education to have any kind of meaningful future.

When I was on the Virginia Board of Education, we could shut schools down that were failing. We could send those students to better-performing schools. I don't think the board has that power anymore, but we had the ability to do that.

My old colleague Bob McDonnell—who was Virginia governor in 2010—appointed me, and then I was approved by the General Assembly.

American public education needs an overhaul, and Virginia could especially use one. When I was serving on the state board, I remember one school system was failing so badly that our board brought the system's *entire school board* to appear before us, the chair and the vice chair, one or two others on the board. The chair kept making excuses. I asked her how long she had been on that board of education.

Nine years, two terms.

The majority were at least two-termers.

The school was failing the whole time that they had been there. You had to believe that *they* were part of the problem.

Our children don't get do-overs. They age, they become adults. They must move out into the world. They get the *one* chance to get a sound education in their youths. After that, it's catch-as-catch-can. Never as good, never as ideal as it could be. You're never eight years old again, ready to take in reading, math, and all the things truly great teachers can teach you.

Before I was on the board, the state had eliminated vocational tracks. One group complained that kids were being tracked due to racism. They claimed some kids were on a college track, while other kids were on a vocational track because of race.

But some children don't want to go to college. Some want to go to college later. Now we see the fruits of this one-track system. Remember, the best welders, carpenters, and so on make a good living!

If you find injustice, you fix it. You keep the two tracks, but fix them so everybody has the opportunity.

One reason that government exists is to make sure the playing field is fair, not to tilt it one way or another. Not to tear down all the goalposts. When you do that, you get chaos, madness, and everybody— Black and White, Asian, Latino, whoever—everyone ends up poorer and cheated out of a good, productive life.

We throw out sense and sensibility at our peril!

* * *

I served on the board for four years. Bob could only serve one term as governor. Virginia limits the governorship to one four-year term with no consecutive terms allowed. After that, Terry McAuliffe, a Democrat, was elected the new governor. I was told that McAuliffe wanted to reappoint me to serve until they found a Democrat to replace me. McAuliffe was advised to let me go, otherwise he would have to allow me to serve the entirety of the new four-year term.

In any case, during those initial four years, the board met once a month in Richmond. I'd drive over from Winchester for these meetings.[1] Most of our formal meetings were preceded by work meetings the day before. These were generally open to interested parties, but nobody was ever there. We may have only met monthly, but I had massive books of information to digest on matters coming before the board. Curriculum decisions, failing schools, school or teacher score cheating and abnormalities, disciplinary measures. If it had to do with Virginia schools, we handled it. We handled the accreditation of the schools of education at colleges and universities. I was soon appointed chair of the lab school subcommittee. After two years I was elected vice president of the board.

One of my biggest contributions was reform of the application process for obtaining a Virginia teacher license. I drew on my work as a delegate reforming those thirteen different medical boards after taking up the JLARC study from where it had been gathering dust. We addressed competency and subject knowledge. We strengthened background investigations. The schools superintendent told me that because I kept singing the praises of the medical boards and the way they now performed their investigations under the new statutes I'd helped make law, she'd hired the best investigator away from the new, reformed medical board!

I was always adamant that we shore up the teachers who were in our classrooms. It's a matter of safety and it's a matter of helping our children to learn. We found teachers who had fudged their previous work, lied about their GPA, lied about actually having degrees.

I always tried to ask of the school superintendent, or the school board chair, or a teacher coming before the board what a *parent* might want to know. I tried to ask what a parent would ask were they sitting in my seat.

Another issue for me was ensuring citizen access to the board. I advocated for the board to meet at least quarterly in Virginia's four corners—which I was told would be a logistical nightmare. We eventually settled on having the public come to town hall board meetings that were held in their neck of the woods and with board members who were able to attend.

* * *

It was an interesting time. I was building my appliance business. Katia and Janel were in college at Virginia Commonwealth University in Richmond. Janel was interested in fashion and design marketing. Janel's fashion sense showed early. She understood and appreciated clothes. From the time she was a toddler, she refused to wear pants! She wanted her pretty dresses. (I don't get it. I wear what's available, and even better if it's pressed! But, as Mark Twain said, "Clothes make the man. Naked people have little influence on society."[2])

Anyhow, after college Janel went to New York to work for a designer. Up there she's been invited to work fashion week five or six years in a row, working behind the scenes to get the organization, the models, and the clothes ready. She eventually moved back down.

Katia got her master's degree in sports management. Her job involves world travel. Prior to that, she stayed in Richmond for a while after college, then moved back to Winchester. And then it was all of us working at Shenandoah Appliance, all three women running our company. From time to time we'd get people calling, they'd hear a woman's voice and instead want to talk to Mr. Sears, Mr. Winston Sears!

When Covid hit, Gov. Ralph Northam, a Democrat, closed the state down. Unlike in Florida, where they discussed how the virus was behaving, adapted, and was overcome, Northam had destroyed with draconian restrictions put in place—and kept in place.

My repair guys were declared "essential." You could be stopped, questioned by the *police*. It was a bad time. The restrictions on customer contact were ridiculously complex.

We got through it. Many did not. We heard of business owners committing suicide. People lost everything, lost their retirement. We did not have to shut down as we did in Virginia.

When the governor gave the approval for us to fully open up, what happened? The government started paying our employees to stay home. Companies cannibalized one another, snatching away employees who did want to work. You can't blame the employees. They'd go to the highest bidder. People who wanted to work were at a premium.

We had a hard time bringing in new employees.

Covid did not make it worse. The decisions of our governor made it worse.

Our governor was a medical doctor. He knew how viruses behave. He knew the science and yet he did not follow it. Look at our current president, Joe Biden. Two vaccines and four boosters, and he still got Covid twice. The president of Pfizer, the CDC director, all came down with Covid. If they'd not politicized the epidemic and made rightfully skeptical citizens out to be the worst people on this Earth, maybe we would still believe in them.

They blamed our students' setbacks in education on the pandemic. Nonsense. It was their reaction, their bad policies that are to blame for that. It was government policy, not Covid, that caused this massive learning loss.[3]

We heard of private schools that opened back up rapidly even as public schools remained closed. I asked one private school headmaster how he'd handled the problem.

"We sent the child home for quarantine. We cleaned up the area, and we started back up," he said. "We can't afford to be closed. We don't get paid to stay home."

We heard of parents who had one child in private school and one child in public school. The child in private school went to school. The child in public school stayed home pecking on a computer, not learning anything.

Our children suffered from mental issues and socialization issues. Our younger children had to keep those masks on, keep them on no matter what, even when they finally went back. They weren't sounding their vowels properly because the masks interfered. I was reading about teachers who didn't even know their students' faces once they took the masks off.[4]

Those government vaccine mandates shred the HIPAA laws to pieces. People were required to disclose their medical history to just about everyone. There were waiters and waitresses in restaurants asking for your vaccination record. Really? This is how overboard we went.

Meanwhile, Florida was thriving.

And throughout 2022, the ultraleft kept harping on racism. Racism, racism, racism. My dad came to America in 1963 when things were *really* bad for Black people. There were real dog whistles, real fire hoses being sprayed at Black people, hotels and restaurants were *actually* segregated.

It's not 1963 anymore.

No, it's 1984. George Orwell's 1984, where they cancel you, they dox you, they send the mob after you.

They can get you fired, destroy your business. Even me, a Black woman. But I'm a Republican. I'm not of the right party. I don't count as Black to them.

The media, the leftist, forget history. After revolutions of this type run out of immediate enemies, they will come for *you*.

So Shenandoah Appliance had the work, but no workers. We ran out of employees. We kept jacking up the hourly wage we paid until it just wasn't economically feasible anymore. We ended up closing out the business. By that time, I'd won my next election.

Chapter Seventeen

REPRESENTING THE CAUSE

In 2018, I had read about an unfortunate occurrence in Chicago's Third Congressional District. A man had gone around saying that he was a Republican. He collected the required amount of signatures and ended up as the nominee for the Republican slot on the ticket. There had been nobody else running.

It turned out this man was a neo-Nazi.[1]

I said to myself that if I lived in that district I would run against him simply to show that his candidacy was not representative of the Republican Party. Somebody there ought to challenge him with a write-in campaign.

That June we had our own nomination battle in Virginia. There were three candidates for the Republican nomination for U.S. Senate, and our nominee ended up being Corey Stewart.

Stewart was a man who had said that a Wisconsin politician who was a self-described White supremacist, antisemite, and apparent American Nazi, Paul Nehlen, was his personal hero.[2] Nehlen was disavowed by every conservative across the spectrum from Paul Ryan to Steve Bannon.[3]

Stewart disavowed him as well. Yet Stewart paid $800 for Nehlen's fund-raising list. I called him out on that. Later Stewart said something I found particularly dangerous. He said that in Virginia when we don't like the status quo we rebel.

He said that we rebelled during the Civil War, and we would do it again.

No!

Democrats rebelled. Not Republicans.

At the time of the Civil War, the Republican Party was the party of Abraham Lincoln and the abolition of slavery. One of its central tenets was opposition to slavery in all its forms. Stewart was supposed to be representing the Republican Party, and here he was saying what? Did the *wrong side* win the Civil War?

I felt that Stewart was not who we Republicans should be putting up for U.S. senator. He'd been elected by only 5.5 percent of Republicans in a crowded primary field. He did not stand for the majority of us.

I heard from many other Republicans quietly that they were ashamed of our nominee. But most didn't want the aggravation of running an opposition.

So I ran as a write-in candidate against him.

I knew that it was the right thing to do. I also knew some were going to be angry with me. I had to follow the urging of my conscience and the Lord. If it's righteous, it's righteous. That's all there is to it.

Corey Stewart didn't have a chance anyway. He'd been burning bridges left and right in the party itself. He had alienated the populist voters who were his original base of voters. Besides, I knew I wasn't going to peel away that many votes from him.

I think I got maybe ten thousand write-in votes in the end.

I wasn't necessarily trying to get votes. I was trying to take a stand.

I was also running because to vote for the Democratic candidate was unthinkable for many people, including myself. Stewart did not represent the values of Republicans.

Unfortunately, Kaine was destined to win.

We had to do better as Republicans not for our sake, but for the sake of the people of Virginia.

* * *

In 2019, Virginia's Democratic governor Ralph Northam was caught in a photo that depicted him either in blackface or under a KKK sheet gazing through eye holes. You couldn't tell which he was in the photo, but it was on a yearbook page from his medical school days *devoted specifically to him*.[4] At first he was described as one of those shown in the photo, then he denied it altogether.

Of course the liberal media rushed to his defense. But Northam went to medical school in his midtwenties, not his teen years. This was an adult man's choice for his party dress.

We have to put an end to it.

That photo demonstrated that Northam had been one of those arrogant, condescending Democrats in training.

The Democrats at first tried to get rid of him. They paid a call upon the lieutenant governor, Democrat Justin Fairfax, a Black gentleman. But Fairfax, it turned out, was accused by two women of sexual assault.[5, 6, 7]

So Fairfax wouldn't do. The Democrats went down the line to the next successor, Attorney General Mark Herring. He was White, but he would have to do.

Wouldn't you know it? It turned out Herring admitted to having partied in blackface as well.[8]

What if all three resigned in ignominy? When Democrats realized that the next in the line of succession would be the Republican speaker of the Virginia House of Delegates, Kirk Cox, suddenly the issue didn't seem so bad.

"Wait a minute! Time-out! Everybody stay in place!"

The Democratic majority was not going to have a Republican as governor. So they forgave all the blackface of the White elected state-wide officials.

Fox News asked me about all of this, the allegations of sexual assault and the racist issue. I said if it's true, then all of them should resign.

What a debacle! What a shame for my dear Commonwealth!

* * *

A lot of people responded to that Fox interview. One of them was Vernon Robinson, the treasurer for the Black Americans to Reelect the President PAC. He called and asked me to become the national chairwoman of his organization.

I prayed about it and agreed to do it.

Trump was a New Yorker. I understood how New Yorkers can be. I was raised in New York. If you look at Alexandria Ocasio-Cortez, she challenges everything. That's what New Yorkers do. That's Chuck Schumer's attitude, as well.

Just about everybody had issues with President Donald Trump's personality, yet he had delivered during his term in office. He told NATO countries that they had to pay their fair share of defense of the continent of Europe, for example. All they had been asked to pay was 2 percent of their GDP. The American taxpayer was picking up the tab for them. He lowered the corporate tax rates for those companies that wanted to bring their overseas profits back to the United States so that they could build *our* economy and create jobs here. That was exactly what they did. We had unprecedented economic activity.[9]

Listen, the so-called Russian dossier turned out to be a fraud. At the present time, nobody's going to jail over that. If they did this to the president of the United States, none of us are safe. Hillary Clinton was caught with classified emails on her personal server, potentially violating national law.[10] FBI director James Comey gave her a frown and a free pass.[11]

Anyway, Trump took on prison reform. People had been talking about it for years; nothing happened. Then along came Trump, and we got the First Step Act signed into law.[12]

He forgave about $360 million that some of the HBCUs owed to the federal government.[13] This was debt that they had carried since Hurricane Katrina days.

The United States had become a net energy producer.[14] Imagine that! We were exporting energy to our allies. Trump's Abraham Accords were put in place,[15] and the foundation for a lasting peace in the Middle East was begun. The list goes on and on. You had to think, well, even if you don't like the man's personality, he's getting the job done. We wish that he had just kept quiet.

But who can forget his reference to "my African-American over there"?[16]

Or Trump saying POW John McCain was not a war hero, or his mocking a handicapped man.[17]

Some may say I should not have supported him, but if God could use Balaam's donkey,[18] then He can use anybody. I thought at some point Trump would become humble.

Second Chronicles 12:12 says, "Because Rehoboam humbled himself, the LORD's anger turned from him, and he was not totally destroyed. Indeed, there was some good in Judah."[19]

This is God coming to the political leader with a moral message about being humble. Was Trump going to be this person? Would he humble himself? That is the key question. Although I'm not looking for a pastor in chief but a commander in chief, still you want the humility.

Unfortunately he didn't keep quiet—that wasn't in his nature— and we are where we are, which is in a much poorer and more dangerous state as a nation. President Joe Biden is a disaster.

* * *

So I decided I'd volunteer when Vernon offered.

We went about raising money, getting to the various communities.

I'd make a speech and somebody would tell me, "You ought to think about running for office." I would pooh-pooh it. No way, that wasn't the mission. I was done with that kind of politics.

We spoke to African American groups, Latino groups, Asian groups. We were not just supporting the president, we were also backing conservative candidates at the same time, especially minority Republicans.

It's very hard for Republican minority candidates to raise money because invariably we are often running in districts that are hard to win. Once again, it's the self-fulfilling prophecy: People think you can't win and so they don't fund you and you usually don't win. What we were trying to do was build the party.

We must bring in more constituents to the Republican Party so that we can have sane and sensible policy in this country. We want to change and build our party, but we don't fund the candidates who can accomplish this. In the meantime you see Democrats swimming in money. They build a farm team and play in Republican districts, trying to hollow them out. Vernon did the logistics work. Vernon is a former Air Force captain and Air Force Academy graduate.[20]

Looking back, the Democrats taught us by way of Bill Clinton that we should ignore a person's private life and concentrate only on his public life. Has that changed now that a candidate is Republican? Double standards abound.

Democrat Richard Blumenthal of Connecticut claims to have been in Vietnam.[21] He still won his election. He's a senator.

The man got five deferments![22]

He intimated that he had been on the battlefield in Vietnam!

We veterans call that stolen valor. I served proudly in the U.S.

Marines, but I don't claim to have been on any foreign battlefields. Stolen valor is no joke among Marines.

I don't know Trump personally, never took a picture with the man. Never spoke to him. For the good of the nation, I do *not* think he should run again in 2024. But while he was in office he had a record I could support.

Double standards still abound. Look at the alleged influence peddling schemes of Hunter Biden.[23] If any Republican had been accused of the things Hunter Biden seems to have done, they wouldn't have had a chance. Not a chance.

What did George Orwell say in *Animal Farm*? "All animals are equal, but some animals are more equal than others."[24]

It's all doublespeak and double standards with those people.

* * *

As I said, people began to suggest that I might run for office at the end of some of my talks. Nobody had asked me to run for a specific position. They just thought that I seemed to have something to say and the ability to do it for the people of Virginia.

So I prayed about it. Nothing happened. Didn't hear a thing, didn't hear a peep.

Then I heard very clearly the Lord say, "You're asking the wrong question. The question is not whether you should run, but whether you are willing to lose. Because if you are willing to lose, you can do anything."

Actually, that answer isn't just for politics. For example, are you willing to challenge your boss because of fraud? You might lose your job, your house.

That was it. If you're willing to lose, then you can do anything.

He was reminding me of Joshua. Joshua was the man who had his soldiers walk around the walls of Jericho, and the walls came tumbling down. But prior to that, Joshua saw a man standing before him with a drawn sword in his hand. It turns out this man was an angel. Joshua went up to him and asked, "Are you for us or for our enemies?"[25]

The angel answers Joshua in a curious manner.

He says "Neither."[26]

This would've been a shock to me if I were Joshua.

"Wait a minute," I might have said. "I'm supposed to go into battle, and now you're telling me you're *not on my side*? I know you say you're not on their side, either, but *I'm* the one who needs the help!"

But no. The question is: Who is on the Lord's side?

Joshua, you're asking the wrong question, the angel is saying.

The angel also chides him a bit, "By the way, take off your sandals. This is holy ground you're standing on."[27]

So that was what the Lord was saying to me. I was asking the wrong question.

If you are willing to lose, you really can do anything. There is a cost to everything that you do. People go into business with no guarantees. They're willing to lose what they put in. They may not realize that they're willing to lose, but those are the stakes; there are opportunity costs. You *will* say things that make some people mad. If you make them mad enough, they may come after you, especially in this day and age of being doxed and canceled.

My dad took a risk in coming to America. He didn't know if he would make it. Black Americans have been doing it since freedom rang. Irish, Italians, you name it, Arabs, everybody.

If you can't make it in America, you can't make it anywhere.

I kept asking, but God had already answered the question.

*   *   *

Why lieutenant governor?

As it turned out, lieutenant governor was a wise choice because at the time we had candidates on our side for governor who all seemed like a capable bunch. I figured I could best fit in as the lieutenant gubernatorial nominee.

I wanted to concentrate on education. I'd served on the State Board of Education. There were so many specifics I knew now about how to bring about reform.

We had critical race theory invading the schools.

Children were not learning anything.

I could also talk about crime, especially as it affects minority communities. The media was telling us that cities being looted, ransacked, and burned down in 2020 wasn't real, when the very buildings were on camera burning in the background behind them. Leftist mayors and city councils were defunding the police. Who are we going to call when we are being mugged, our children shot, our houses invaded. We saw smash-and-grabs at stores and pharmacies, and somehow this was supposed to be social justice. Black neighborhoods were burning down. There was political unrest everywhere. Our society was degrading before our very eyes.

And it was alleged that BLM people were raking in money in the millions and spending it on themselves.[28]

George Floyd died when he should be on Earth today because a bad cop was on his neck. Should he have gotten a death sentence for passing the fake $20 bill? Absolutely not!

Nothing made sense. And the governor of Virginia was shutting down houses of worship because of Covid policies. What did he mean by doing that? He was telling us *how* we were going to worship, and that the government had final say on the manner in which we worshipped. Only so many can gather. This is where you can gather, and how you can gather, and how long.

It was pure dystopian authoritarianism.

He also shut our businesses down. There are justifiable permitting processes and OSHA inspections, but this was different. This was total control of human enterprise. He shut down our schools. All of this was unprecedented. We didn't do this sort of thing even in Spanish flu times, a much worse epidemic to hit America.

The whole country, it seemed, was coming apart. Government had taken unto itself powers it shouldn't have had.

* * *

The election came and went. President Trump lost. I still felt I did not have a definitive answer from the Lord. Yes, I was willing to lose, but what was I to do?

Meanwhile, my husband had been saying to me, "You know you want to get back in."

I'd say no, and he'd say, "Yeah, you miss it."

He had been saying that throughout our years in Winchester. This was a totally different reaction than he'd had when I'd run for the U.S. Congress.

I figured perhaps I'd better listen to the man.

Nah! I decided not to run.

All was right until about six o'clock that night. I was cleaning up and I saw a copy of a messianic magazine that I had not read. I flipped through the pages. There was this Scripture from Philippians:

Don't be afraid of your opponents; always be courageous, and this will prove to them that they will lose and that you will win, because it is God who gives you the victory. For you have been given the privilege of serving Christ, not only by believing in him, but also by suffering for him. Now you can take part with me in the battle. It is the same battle you saw me fighting in the past, and as you hear, the one I am fighting still.[29]

What struck me was the word "suffering."

Suffering. I don't want to suffer. I've been there and have suffered enough already. I'm too old for this. Twenty years before, I had also challenged the then-Republican Speaker of the House.

Then I heard the Lord's voice so clearly and He said, "It's even deeper than that. Are you willing to be *eaten*?"

Eaten.

Once I heard Him say that word, I knew clearly what He meant. I had been reading about Daniel. Like I said, I try to read the Bible through every year. But I've done it so many times, I don't do it sequentially anymore. Sometimes I do it topically. Sometimes I order my reading as the mood or moment strikes me.

So I was reading in Daniel at that time.

I asked, "Lord, how does Daniel become Daniel? No matter what You say to him, Daniel *does* it. You tell him to go tell the people something, he *does* it. He's not full of fear. Where does a man like this come from? What is it about Daniel that I'm missing? I want to be like Daniel."

The Lord answered me clearly. "Daniel was willing to be eaten."

I had been reading about the lions' den. Wicked Babylonian politicians knew Daniel's character was impeccable, so they thought they'd use that against him. They came up with a trap. All he had to do was not pray to God, or at least not be caught praying to God, and he'd be safe.

The minute that the law was passed, Daniel went up into his house to pray in the same way that he always had. He didn't miss a beat. He opened the windows to the heavens and the people saw him, and the politicians said, "Yes, we've got him now!"

Daniel had a great relationship with the emperor (the politician), and they were jealous. The emperor did all he could to avoid throwing Daniel to the lions. Ultimately, though, he was caught in the logic of his own words. He had to do it.

When the Lord said, "It's even deeper than that. Are you willing to be eaten?" I understood exactly what He meant.

To be like Daniel, I must face that lion's den.

I must not merely be willing to lose, but to be consumed. I was not naïve. I'd been through the wringer. I knew what could happen.

But so much needed to be accomplished. So many could be helped. Here was the chance.

I was going to run for lieutenant governor.

Chapter Eighteen

THE NOMINATION

I had been folding laundry. I got up and went out to my family in the living room. They were gathered in front of the television. I said to them, "Guess who is running for lieutenant governor?" I told them how the Lord had spoken to me.

The faces of my children fell. They knew what it had been like when I ran for delegate. They had been exposed to death threats. They had been exposed to people who hated me and consequently hated them. They were young at the time, but they remembered. My girls were afraid for us.

On the other hand, they were both now grown women, proudly independent and no longer as vulnerable as they once had been. I resolved to keep them out of what was to come as much as possible.

I had a big problem almost immediately. I needed a campaign manager, and most of them were already with the other candidates. I cast about, and Vernon Robinson told me about a young man who seemed qualified but somewhat inexperienced. I didn't know him.

I reached out and I had a long talk about all manner of things, some not political. I wanted to know who he was, so we discussed where we were in our faith. I explained to him how I went about things, that my decisions were grounded in prayer, and I might make decisions that he wouldn't necessarily understand, but I believed I was following the Lord's path.

I told him, You have to have a strong faith to work with me sometimes. I will take risks. You have to trust me.

He considered and said, "Okay, I'm along for the ride."

I told him it might be a wild one. Indeed it was.

That was November 2020. I was trying to find an opportune time to announce but it was Christmas. Then we were into the new year. I originally considered early January. But during the certification of the Electoral College results on the presidential election, there were protests in Washington, DC.

Rioters smashed into the Capitol Building, creating chaos, creating fear, destroying government property, in order to push Vice President Mike Pence not to certify the election. My first thought was, We can't have this. If we don't like our government, we vote them out. You can't go in and smash things; the taxpayer is going to have to pay for this. These actions are un-American.

No, I did not agree with those methods whatsoever, and I thought the people engaged in them were unhinged.

This also changed my announcement plan. There was no way to cut through the wall-to-wall coverage of the riot.

I finally announced January 16. This wasn't ideal, but I couldn't keep putting it off. All but one of my eventual opponents had already announced. Some had been campaigning since September. I couldn't let any more time go by, or the field would be set without me. That might work for some latecomers, but I was an unknown who had been out of office for twenty years.

Most of the state-level Republican endorsements were gone. Most of the money was gone. If there was an establishment, they weren't interested in me. But I was confident. I knew that this was what I should do.

We put the announcement first on YouTube.

My campaign manager brought with him a team, some freelancers, several consultants. This team put together a video, and that's how we did it. We posted it on social media.

Where did the money come from, you might ask. Me. It cost $10,000.

We followed up with press releases and appearances. There was a moment of held breath, however. Then a few key Republicans took it up, realizing I was serious. Whether they wanted me in the race or not, they saw they were going to have to deal with me.

From that moment, we built the campaign. It took a while making calls, knocking on doors, and simply asking for what we needed to get going. We were able to pay our bills soon enough.

I'm trying to build our party, I told whoever would listen. The whole state had gone Democrat the last two cycles. We must not keep losing or we will fade to irrelevance. We cannot let that happen. The stakes are too great. Our children aren't learning. Our economy is in shambles. Our police are demoralized.

I know how to reach the new folks, I said to them. I can speak to new voters who need to hear our message, who are waiting to hear our message if they only can be reached. The dead canary in the mine was telling us Republicans something. Republicans, you are *not* winning statewide elections. We placated ourselves over many years with the idea that at least we had won the House and Senate in the General Assembly.

Then we lost those.

The Democrats, who had been taken over at the top by hard left-ists, started passing insane laws with their majority.

We needed not just to bring out the base; we needed *new* voters. We would get the whole party out, but there simply weren't enough people, even when combined with independents who might vote with us. We *had* to grow the party.

There are multitudes of Black people and other minority people who agree with our positions. Of course they did, because we were the party of common sense, law and order, economic sanity, righteousness when it came to the right to life.

These communities knew they weren't being served by the Democrats. They needed to know they were welcome in the Republican Party.

I was a messenger, a *good* messenger, a *believable* messenger. My running for lieutenant governor was an *opportunity* for the party, if they would only see that.

*   *   *

The primary campaign was a long, hard slog. I was at first the only woman in the primary race. I was running against the "fellows," as I liked to call them.

We hit the trail.

I'd learned from the best to ask the question, "What would I want to hear if I were the people I'm speaking to? What are *their* wants and needs *right now*, today, this hour?"

Most of all, I had a calling, a plan, and a message.

I also had a great and humbling task before me: build the party, bring in people we might never have reached before.

Republicans tell parents that they, not the government, are in charge of their children. Parents not only want that responsibility, they demand it.

It was immediately apparent that I was intriguing audiences with this message. All of us primary candidates would go together to the local GOP units. There was a veritable caravan of us. Coming along with us were the gubernatorial candidates, and attorney general candidates, all of the statewide primary slate. There were eight people running for the gubernatorial nomination, a huge field.

My opponents for the lieutenant governor nomination were former delegate Tim Hugo, current delegate Glenn Davis, Lance Allen, an Air Force vet, and Puneet Ahluwalia, an Indian immigrant who had come to America with nothing and ended up a great businessman. He'd reached the American dream.

We were all Republicans, so we all believed in pretty much the same values. Small government. Fair taxes. Taxpayer money for roads, medical, education, yes. Money spent wisely. Education, not indoctrination in toxic leftist ideologies. Law and order. And more education on top of that!

We stood for the freedom to worship in the way we wish. Government must stay out of religion.

Free enterprise. People making their own economic decisions. A society of law and order.

The candidates' views were sound. What we needed was someone who could win.

We were losing, and I was tired of losing.

Who among us could bring in the new voters we were going to need?

That would be me.

I have the strategy and, frankly, I *look* like the strategy. I'm a woman. I'm Black. I'm an immigrant. I'm a veteran. I'm a small business owner. There it is.

If the Democrats and their media accused me of not caring about the poor, hang on, my dad came here with $1.75 in his pocket. If they accused me of not caring about those who have been through rough times, wait a minute, you're looking at somebody who lost her home to foreclosure. I don't care about the poor? I ran a homeless shelter. I care about the incarcerated. I sacrifice my time to bring a message of hope every Wednesday at six o'clock to a prison ministry near Winchester.

I know about building a business from scratch. I was still a Jamaican citizen when I joined the Marines, and I was willing to give my life for this country then, and after I became a naturalized citizen. When the Marine Corps puts a rifle in your hand and tells you this is your best friend, you understand what trade you're in now.

* * *

The GOP units would coordinate to some extent so we could be in the area at the same time. That way, people could come out and hear from all of us.

So you'd see the caravan, car upon car, driving along Virginia's highways and back roads to one meeting, then on to the next. And the next day, we'd do it all over again. We got to hear one another's speeches over and over again. After a while, each of us could pretty much give the other's stump speech from memory. Along the way, we had heard about this one guy who might join the race, a mystery candidate who might come on board.

It turned out to be Glenn Youngkin. Soon he was in the gubernatorial race.

Then, on the day before the last day that you could file to be a candidate, a woman turned up running for lieutenant governor. This was Maeve Rigler. We would just have to outwork everybody. Listen, no hard feelings. Everyone wants to win. Politics is brutal. It's not a lovefest. But after the play is called, we come together.

* * *

Initially, we were given ten minutes to speak on these caravan stops. The organizers quickly discovered that that was not a good idea with eight people running for governor, six running for lieutenant governor, and another four running for attorney general. It went down to five minutes, and finally—

"Two minutes! Two minutes! Everybody's got two minutes!"

We went to the Republican women's clubs, we went to conservative associations. We went to Tea Party groups. We weren't speaking to a wider audience yet. That would come later. We were vying to get the nomination.

The Democrats had their own primary field. They had their own set of problems to deal with. Among their gubernatorial candidates were two Black females running for governor, and Terry McAuliffe, of course. This was a big problem for a party tearing itself apart with identity politics. They weren't worried about us yet.

* * *

During the cycle, we were on our way to a GOP meeting when we passed a rifle range.

It had been a while since I'd been at the range.

So we stopped by Clark Brothers Range in Warrenton, Virginia. I put on a green coat to keep the spent gunpower blowback off my blouse.

When you look at the photo taken there, you can see that I still have my earplugs in. Nothing staged there.

The picture took off. It went viral.

It's not as if an AR is unknown to me. In the Marines I had an M-16. I had to break the thing down and put it back together. There's a photo of me with my M-16 in full battle dress, my helmet, my camouflage, my flak jacket, my extra magazines, everything. I look ready to go, because I was. We were engaging in a war game at the time. So standing with that AR was normal and natural for me.

I think it's pretty powerful, a Black woman standing with a gun like that.

Furthermore, because of all the mayhem that antifa and their ilk had been raining down on the country, Black women were buying more guns than ever before. Black women are now the fastest growing group of gun owners in our society. Women were buying guns, yes, but a particular set of women—Black women—were buying the most.[1]

The first laws against gun ownership were against Black people owning guns. I'm a Black woman and I'm not giving up my Second Amendment rights. Harriet Tubman carried a gun, and if a gun was good enough for her, it's good enough for me. Part of being a law-abiding citizen is the right to bear arms.

Plus, Democrats are often hypocrites, surrounded by people with guns who protect them. Some of these, including female Democrat congresswoman Cori Bush, have hired security teams who carry guns.[2]

Dr. Martin Luther King Jr. himself applied for a carry permit in 1956 for self-protection, but was denied by the State of Alabama.[3]

They're telling other Black women *we* can't have guns? No way I'm listening to that.

* * *

The primary seemed to be going well. But you can't know for sure. I had been gone from politics for twenty years. I would call Republican politicians only to discover that they had already endorsed another before I got into the race. I told them, You gave your word. I don't hold anything against you. The other candidates are good people, so if you remove your endorsement, I'd think less of you.

The Republican convention was May 8, 2021. Republicans voted on Friday and Saturday. I had started out in Loudoun County, because that's my voting precinct for the convention. I hung around there for several hours encouraging people to vote for me as the cars would come through. Then we moved on to Fairfax County.

There I saw Glenn Youngkin and some of my opponents. I had planned to go down to Prince William County and finish the day. But there were so many cars at Fairfax that I decided to stay there. Glenn stayed, too. So we closed out the day canvassing.

Then it was done. It was over.

We Republicans used a new process of ranked choice voting in the primary. Many of us didn't understand it well.[4] The idea was to avoid what had happened previously with Corey Stewart and get, we hoped, more representative candidates. You would vote for your first choice, your second, third, fourth, fifth, and sixth, ranking your vote.[5]

The first round of counting went through. Below a certain threshold, candidates fell away. Then those candidates' votes would be distributed among the remaining candidates during a new count. Then the next two would be dropped, and so on, until they found the winner.

They started counting with the attorney general candidates. It was a nailbiter. Eventually Jason Miyares was chosen. Then it went on to the gubernatorial count, another nailbiter. I don't remember how many rounds they went, maybe five rounds, until we found out it was to be Glenn Youngkin.

Now for my race. I survived the first round. I was number one. In the ballot listing, I had been the sixth candidate down. I had complained to the Lord, "Wait a minute, You put me at the bottom of the list!"

You had to go all the way down the ballot to get to my name and choose me for number one. My strategy when talking with voters was to say to them, well, if you can't make me your number one pick, then make me your number two. Go for your number one, but at least consider me for your number two choice.

Anyway, for the first round, I had 33 percent of the vote. Maeve was the first to go. Her votes were reassigned. This was where the second choice, the number twos, became important. The second round I survived again. I was on top. Puneet and Lance were the next to go. Along came the next round, and Glenn Davis was out. It was now between Tim Hugo and me.

That night, I had made my way from Winchester down to Richmond where the ballots were being counted. Some of my opponents had been there from the time they started counting the attorney general race.

I had things to do at my house. I needed to get the place in order after being away. I still had my business, which I was in the process of winding down.

I had been planning to head to the convention location later in the day, but I got a call that the race had been called at ten o'clock that morning and it looked like I had won.

But no—mistake! The counting needed a do-over. The votes were still being allocated. It was not until about six o'clock that night that it was finally decided.[6]

I had won the nomination.

I made a short speech to the convention delegates, thanking them. I also told them they owed me a stomach, because they'd just about yanked mine out that day. My campaign manager and I walked arm in arm and talked about how far we'd come. Here I was coming back after almost a twenty-year absence from politics. Moses came back after forty years. I came back after twenty. Just call me "Little Mo."

But I also said to them, you're looking at a walking impossibility, according to some. I shouldn't be here. I shouldn't be in this position. I'm an immigrant. I was a little Black girl who stepped off a plane into a different culture. Now here I am the Republican nominee for the lieutenant governor of the Commonwealth of Virginia. The first minority woman nominated in a Virginia statewide race.

Who in their right mind would have ever believed this could be true? Only in America.

Chapter Nineteen

HOW SWEET IT IS!

Now the fight was truly beginning. Apparently, once again, I wasn't Black enough.[1,2]

But, you know, with some ultraleftists if you're not a Democrat you're never Black enough.

They said it twenty years ago and here they were saying it again. It's just a broken record. After a while you're inoculated against it. The insult has lost whatever meaning they hoped it had.

There are Black people who vote for me. Those who fling the lie are insulting those people, as well.

For what purpose? Is Blackness granted by leftists? Are they the ones who granted me my skin color?

No, it was God who made that decision.

What they are really saying is that all Black people should think alike. You know who put it explicitly? Joe Biden. Remember that "you ain't Black" if you don't vote for him comment?[3]

And in case you think that was a one-off, what about when he was addressing the National Association of Black Journalists and National Association of Hispanic Journalists Joint Virtual Convention in 2021?

"Unlike the African American community, with notable exceptions, the Latino community is an incredibly diverse community, with incredibly different attitudes about different things. It's a very diverse community."[4]

We Black people suffer insult upon insult. We are not afraid anymore to speak our minds. We never should have been afraid. We're adults. Not all feel this way, but some Black Democrats have appointed themselves leaders over us, and if you don't keep in line, then they are going to cast you out.

Well, too late. It's a healthy thing for Black people to be on both sides of the political spectrum.

* * *

So I was the nominee. Time to close ranks in the Republican family. That didn't mean more money. It was still a difficult slog. You have to remember what we as Republicans were coming out of—a political black hole. Republicans had lost the presidency in 2020, and we had lost the two U.S. Senate races in Georgia. It was a terrible time for Republicans.

And here comes President Biden with his policies undoing the gains we had made. He shut down oil pipelines. He swung wide the gates of our borders. He loaded us down with new and pointless regulations. He was playing footsie with Iran. And so much horror was still to come. The debacle and defeat in Afghanistan were around the corner, for example. The media was playing right along, as is their wont. He could do no wrong in their eyes.

So as a party we were as deflated as a flat tire. What I kept hearing was, "Winsome, we spent so much money, hundreds of millions of dollars, and for what? We lost everything. There is no hope. Virginia is a blue state. You can't win. None of you can win."

I had to remind them that if we do nothing then this will be a foregone conclusion, a self-fulfilling prophecy. And if we do that, the Democrats will win again and nothing will change. We will slide into the malaise and degradation of states like California and New York, where crime is rampant, homeless are camped on the streets, and public education is failing our children.

If we want change, we've got to work for it. We've got to spend money to get elected. I'm willing to put myself out there, to put everything into this. I'll take the insults, the attacks. But I need your help to fund the campaign.

I needed help to buy ads. I needed help with gas money to get to the meetings. I needed help to keep the campaign staff and volunteers fed.

I ran the campaign out of my house, just as I had originally run my business from my home. We never got a campaign headquarters. Very quickly the general campaign began to take shape.

We put together the researchers. We made a website. We got our tax ID. We targeted our post cards. We put in phones. I brought in another team. We did the best we could with the little money we had.

* * *

You don't realize how big Virginia is until you start running for office and you're driving it. I remember one day I started in Winchester, drove down to Richmond for a meeting, crossed over to Interstate 64, then to Interstate 81 ... where did I end up? Harrisonburg. Then drove back the same day.

During that time, I had to prepare for speeches and get-togethers, to answer all manner of questions both national and local.

The campaign was a different beast from the campaigns I had when running for the House of Delegates or even a congressional district. It's the whole vast Commonwealth!

That's also one of the beauties of running for statewide office. You see the rolling hills. You see the wide-open spaces. You see the beautiful Virginia countryside. You get to know the routes that people travel. You go to cities and towns you've never been in. Take Fincastle. It's in Botetourt County, north of Roanoke. It's a small town, but a town with a deep history in Western Virginia. The people are simply the salt of the earth. I'd never heard of Fincastle before the campaign. I'd

never been through there. But now I know the people and the place—
and am richer for it.

Then you get to Northern Virginia, and you see so many people
compacted in such a small area, the traffic, and also the excitement of
those cities.

You see the greatness of Virginia, but you also see the problems.
When you have to drive, you get to know the lay of the land. I can't
imagine how the politicians did it back before there were cars and only
horses and buggies. It must've been grueling in the snow, in the rain,
on bumpy roads, on plank and cobblestone roads.

It is grueling enough driving a modern vehicle.

Looking back, I wouldn't trade any of that statewide campaigning for the world. This is how you get to know your Commonwealth.
You're making stops at almost every town. You stop and you go into,
say, a diner, or a hair salon and say, "Hi, I'm Winsome Sears, and I'm
running for lieutenant governor."

Sometimes they look at you with confusion or bewilderment—
sometimes even with disdain. But sometimes you see hope. Who is
this strange lady? You sit down and talk. And most important of all—
you listen. You listen to the people and their concerns. Then you get
up, and you carry on to the next town and do it again.

When I started, I read the newspapers, I listened to the news, I
studied the issues. I generally knew what was on everybody's mind,
because that was what was on my mind.

That's what causes people to run for office. If people are happy with
the status quo, we would just leave it be. Clearly, there were general,
statewide problems. But they came into crystal clear focus when I saw
how they affected individual lives.

Governor Northam had shut us down with the Covid excuse as if
he had been made king. He continued to keep us shut down. It cost
people their jobs. It cost people the family business. It took a terrible
toll on our children's education.

There's mayhem in the streets. People understand peaceful protesting. But there is a way to protest and that is not to set fire to cities and attack the police and regular citizens trying to go about their lives. Yes, in every profession there are bad apples, bad teachers, bad police, bad doctors, and so on. We don't throw out the good with the bad! No! Then it is not protest anymore. It's not justice or seeking justice. It's wrong.

You say you love Black people? You're destroying everything they've worked for when you burned down their businesses.

Yes, it's very educational to drive the state and listen to people with tears in their eyes lamenting the school closures, the devastation this wrought on the education of their children. Or someone telling you their husband, son, daughter, cousin is a police officer. I would hear this refrain, "I fear every day for his safety."

There is no economy without the rule of law. Plus, the economy was *still* shut down in so many places by stupid government rules, incredibly self-defeating payouts. We must restore our economy.

And the biggest issue of all? Education and parental rights.

Our children must have a future. Everything else depends on that. In Charlottesville, for example, the Charlottesville public school system had declared that 80 percent of the children were gifted. Amazing, right? But strangely enough only 50 percent of their children could pass the state standards exam.

Who were they fooling? In the name of social justice they lowered the scores that children need to pass and thus the knowledge you need to be truly educated.[5] These children were lulled into complacency with a pat on the back, a fake trophy.

It is a sin to lie to children. The kids know it deep down, too. It eats away at their sense of worth. It demeans and diminishes the activity that they're participating in. Life doesn't set the standards low. Life tests us. Reality tests us. We need education to triumph at life. It was time for common sense to come back into the school building because she had walked out in disgust.

Parents were figuring this out in record numbers. Governor Northam's policies had shut down in-person schooling, and parents were watching what was going on in the classroom on the computer screens. They were appalled.

How was having a mom and a dad in the home something called "White privilege"?

How did having been in our country's military make somebody an oppressor?

Activist teachers were dividing the children, condemning their parents and relatives. What did any of this have to do with history? With English? With math? Many kids were asking their parents why White people were so bad. And this included themselves or their friends who were White. They were being taught hate. Black children were taught they were victims.

Of course the media and Democrats set up a chorus of disdain. Those Republicans are lying. We're not teaching *that*! There is no critical race theory in the classroom!

We found that many school systems had received taxpayer money for CRT instruction and seminars.[6] School boards were not merely going along, they were instigating and cheering this nonsense on. Our own Board of Education had put it on their website that schools should be teaching critical race theory. Books were recommended, curricula advanced.[7]

They called this teaching history? How? It's activist Marxism. It creates chaos. It isn't teaching. It's indoctrination. It's the difference between learning how to think for yourself and being told what to think.

Power is all that matters in this indoctrination technique—not education, understanding, working together, competition, hope, love, or belief in God. All of that is illusion, in this view. Only power relationships matter.

There was always that word, "privilege." If you are privileged, you have gained power by harming others. You are bad. You are evil. You are to be despised.

If you're White, you're privileged? If you're heterosexual—they call it cisgender—you're privileged? If you're *married* to somebody of the opposite sex, that's privilege?! They say we must teach these things to all our children.[8] That *that's* what education is for, in fact.

No. This is teaching everyone to hate. It's fomenting chaos. And who will step in as the savior? The Marxists. Who wants to live under Marxism? We've seen the kind of police states and despotic regimes Marxists create in this world.

These are the folks who call wrong right. Up is called down. Two plus two equals whatever you want it to equal. Everything, especially the education of the young, is in service to this power-mad ideology.

No. This is America. We're not doing that.

Education is where the rubber meets the road. These parents who observed what was going on and spoke out were the alarm bells, the sirens, of free society.

They said, "No! This is my child. I'm not going to stand for it!"

You had thousands of parents who had formerly been Democrats come over to the Republican side. You can talk about party loyalty all you want, but when it comes to *my* child, all bets are off, baby. If my child isn't learning, I don't care if you are Democrat, Republican, Green Party, or Reform Party, we've got problems.

Enough of these parents who were Democrats, independent-leaning Democrats, and others were saying no, something's got to change. Many Democrats began to realize that the revolution had started to come for them and their families, too. They may have thought, "Hey, I'm safe; I'm a Democrat."

That stopped working.

No. You're still White. Or still married. Still believe family is essential and important. You are now the enemy of the system. Parents are the enemy.

* * *

To top it all off, Merrick Garland, our United States attorney general, sicced Biden's Department of Justice,[9] even sicced FBI agents in person,[10] on Virginia *parents*.

There was one father whose daughter had allegedly been sexually assaulted by another male teen who, according to the victim's father, wore a dress to enter the girl's bathroom. That's where the assault occurred. He was using the same bathroom as the man's daughter.[11] The school board allegedly was unaware.[12]

As any father should, the father came to the school board meeting to tell them that they needed to give him an answer. He demanded to know how that could have happened. And they had law enforcement drag him out.[13]

It was an onslaught of hateful, antidemocratic ideology. It was anti-human and antifamily. In some cases it was just simply disgusting.[14] We discovered that school libraries possessed pornographic books, and teachers were promoting these and other books, these books were nothing less than filth.[15] Not just in high schools, which would be bad enough, but in elementary[16] and middle schools.[17] Pictures of people having sex. Blow jobs. Penises erect. And the language was astonishing.[18] To say these books were unsuitable for children is the understatement of the century.

They were unsuitable for education.

Parents came to school board meetings and read from these books, and in one case the reader was stopped by a school board member. It was too pornographic![19]

* * *

This groundswell grew. I had already been talking about education. Our children weren't learning. By the fourth grade, 45 percent of Asian children could not do math at their age level, along with 59 percent of White children, *80* percent of Latino children and *84* percent of Black children.[20] And they almost never catch up. So there was nothing to crow about. Those statistics are horrific.[21]

Glenn Youngkin and I were on the same wavelength on this, as was our attorney general nominee, Jason Miyares. The lieutenant gubernatorial candidate in Virginia is not chosen by the governor. Nevertheless, Glenn Youngkin from the start included Jason and me in his campaign. This was important to get-out-the-vote efforts. He called Jason and me to coordinate via Zoom on a regular basis.

By that time, we were a tight unit. Like I said, we could finish one another's stump speeches. Glenn was the leader, as he should be.

The first thing Glenn said was, "Let's pray." That impressed me. It had been all politics so far, and I hadn't seen that side of him before. I was very glad of it. He prayed for peace, he prayed for the campaign and the voters. He prayed for us to know how to lead. Prayed for our safety on the trail. And finally he prayed for our great Commonwealth, for we wished to represent everyone in Virginia, and were determined to do so if we won.

* * *

My opponent was incredibly well funded. Wow, did she have money.

Running as a Republican in Virginia, Democrats will always be able to outspend you. They have outside money. They receive tech money, Hollywood money. Money, money, money. And of course they have the entire media corps on their side, with very few exceptions, which produces reams of "free" press. They also have union contributions raked from the dues of members, no matter those members' actual political wishes.

Most Republicans in Virginia know that Democrats will outspend you. They have access to money Republicans do not.

So it should not come as a surprise that my opponent, Hala Ayala, raised nearly $7 million to my $3 million total.[22] Two weeks *prior* to early voting, which is itself forty-five days from election day, she was already up on TV and on radio in the expensive Washington, DC, market, which broadcasts to the northern Virginia area. She had the money. And these were not innocuous advertisements touting her ideas. No, they were attack ads.

I was in the hole about $100,000-plus. Frankly, I had no hope.

And what commercials they were that she ran. They were directed specifically against *me* as a person. They accused me of all manner of vile beliefs, and terrible acts. They impugned my character. They went for the Uncle Tom canard, accusing me of betraying Black people. They were vile. They were ugly. It was clear they were scared to death of me, a Black, woman, immigrant Republican, and were pulling out all the stops. They accused me of leading the January 6 riot. Me! Me, who was horrified by what happened.

So I started praying again. This time I prayed what you might call Davidic prayers. Now King David was many things. He was beloved of God, yes, but he was also very human. David would have had no qualms in praying for his favorite football team to triumph over their rival. He often prayed for the defeat of his enemies in the most graphic manner imaginable.

I prayed for specific outcomes. "Lord, please let her commercials backfire."

It sounds harsh, but what else could I pray? Her commercials were lies and half-truths. I didn't have the money to counter her pernicious nonsense. Indeed, I heard from quite a few people after the election that my prayers were answered. I was out shopping after the election trying not to be recognized. I'd just been all over the news, and I wanted to have a little downtime. But a woman saw me, did a double take, and came up to me.

"Are you Winsome Sears?"

"Yes, ma'am."

"I just wanted to tell you, when you were running for office, I never knew anything about you. I never saw any of your commercials. But I saw your opponent's ads, and it drove me to your website because I thought, No, she couldn't be as bad as they are making her out to be. And I ended up voting for you."

Most of her campaign was attack ads. Every now and then you would see a commercial that wouldn't be. It got so bad that one of the Democrats who was running for delegate to the house attacked *me* in his commercials. He figured he would get on board, I guess.

I thought this was a little unfair. "Hey buddy, you *have* your own opponent in your race!"

But the strategy was to turn me into an object of derision and hate. I was a threat to the base of the Democrats and they knew it.

I didn't have the money for polling. Those internal polls are about $30,000 per poll. I needed the money I did have to go on television and radio. And of course I needed money to pay my professional staff. The national Republican Lieutenant Governors Association helped. They took up my cause and began to put out commercials for me. South Carolina senator Tim Scott did a buy for me in the expensive Washington, DC, market, which would help me to get to northern Virginia.[23] I think that was almost a million-dollar buy. I could never have paid for that, and I was very grateful.

A month after the general campaign started, media polls were showing that I was down ten points. We kept slogging through, slogging through. Slowly but surely, the polls started showing that I was cutting her lead. I was down three points. For the longest time, I couldn't seem to move up. Three points down. Three points down.

Then a poll appeared showing me two points up. I didn't believe it.

You've got to keep going. You've got to keep running like an under-dog. Anything can happen. The only poll that matters is election day.

* * *

Prayer was essential. As a matter of fact, we had a veritable platoon of prayer warriors on the team. This all started at a restaurant, of all places. I casually knew the owner because when I was on the State Board of Education his store was the halfway point from my house to the meeting, and I would normally stop and get a sandwich, get refreshed, and head back out.

So I got to the restaurant, and there sat a woman who had just come back from Israel. She'd been living there for five years.

Out of the blue, she looked me up and down and said, "I want to talk with you. I have a word from the Lord for you."

I thought, Well, this is curious. So I sat down with her and she just began to prophesy, telling me everything about me, what was going to happen in the campaign, and I sat listening dumbfounded. So much of what she said was spot on!

My campaign manager had arrived, and he looked like he was in shock. How could the woman know *specific plans*? She was a prophet.

She didn't tell me I would win! Oh, no. She was there to let me know I was on the right track.

Sometimes that's all you need to go on with your journey. You need strength, you need encouragement, you need hope—even if you're going to lose.

So this lady formed my prayer team. I met another woman through her. First it was just her. She's White. The next lady was Black. Another woman came on who was a Jamaican immigrant. People who were rural and urban joined. Pretty soon we had quite the spiritual unit.

I tell you the races to show that we are simply...people!

They would meet every morning at eight o'clock by conference call and pray. Sometimes I would be on the call with them, sometimes I couldn't. But they were always there. It was so comforting knowing that there were people praying for me. Frequently their prayers lasted an hour, sometimes an hour and a half. They were praying and they *meant* it.

* * *

We did finish my campaign in the black. We paid our bills.

We began to get more media attention. We'd had some throughout the campaign, a local station here and there.

Then the *Washington Post* did a profile[24] that was quite refreshing. Some of the more conservative media outlets like Newsmax and Fox would give me coverage.

My husband, Terry, was my rock. He's been down this road before.

He would give me a quiet "You've got this, babe" just when I needed it.

Terry has a full-time job, of course, but he was able to help. He would stand in for me at speaking engagements I couldn't make. He represented me at many events. He did what all spouses do for candidates, but he has a husbandly way of doing this that is very effective. I was rarely home, but this time we didn't have small children. In my previous campaign, he had very much looked after the family. He still did so, but now our daughters were quite capable of taking care of themselves.

Glenn Youngkin invited all of us to be part of his victory party. I had planned to have my own separate election night event, but decided to accept Glenn's offer. We took him up on his offer. I had a separate suite for me and my folks, but because the results were coming in so slowly we chucked mine, and all my volunteers went down to Youngkin headquarters. So he and I were in the war room together watching the results come in.

The place was abuzz with people. I saw Senator Ted Cruz milling about there, shook his hand. So many other people. We're all dressed up, ready, waiting, waiting, waiting. I hadn't had much sleep. The day before, Youngkin had taken Jason Miyares, me, previous Republican governors, and the Virginia Republican Party chairman on a plane, and we'd done a Commonwealth fly-around, visiting the major stops in Virginia that last day.

I sipped my homemade concoction,[25] trying not to catch anything from exhaustion—no colds, no coughs, no flu—marshaling my strength as best I could. There were bags under my eyes, but nothing a little makeup couldn't fix. I had done all I could. Now the voters would decide.

Our last stop on the plane flight was Leesburg, so we flew there afterward. It was cold and the crowd was huge. It was late at night. Youngkin gave his rally cry, and we all got up onstage. It was our last appeal, our last encouragement and exhortation to the faithful to get out and vote.

Then it was done. We scattered to our homes. The next morning election day dawned.

Now in the war room there fell a sort of calm even among all the chaos. We had taken an early lead, the whole statewide Republican team. We were seemingly ten points ahead. We knew it wouldn't hold.

We watched as it seemed we were 90,000 votes ahead. This total came down to 80,000. Then it came down to 70,000. We were waiting for Northern Virginia to come in. Northern Virginia overwhelmingly votes Democrat. Republicans had been losing northern Virginia 70–30 lately.

We could lose the whole kaboodle in Northern Virginia.

We could win the rest of the state, but if we lost big in Northern Virginia, it would be over. If we could whittle the ratio down to a 60–40 deficit, we would win. We would make it up elsewhere.

The results came in. Our numbers were coming down, coming down.

But then the decrease stopped.

I felt like I was waiting and waiting. Terry and my daughters were there. You're half not believing it. You're half exhausted. Can it be right? No. Somebody's going to find some votes somewhere. We'd have to take it all back.

But after a while it's still holding. Nobody's taking it back. They are not finding any anomalies. It's then that I felt the weight of office on me. You're representing the needs, the hopes, of 8.5 million people.

It became clear that there was no mathematical way my opponent could win.

We'd done it.

It was the reverse of what happened during the primaries at the convention. My election was decided first.

I had won the lieutenant governorship.

Chapter Twenty

A JOB TO DO

It took a while for the other results to arrive. Glenn's numbers came in next. He had won. He would be our governor. Then Jason's numbers arrived. He had also won. He was the first Latino to be elected to Virginia statewide office. It was a clean sweep for our statewide ballot. We had also regained the House of Delegates. Democrats still controlled the Senate, which was not up for election until 2023.

We glanced over at coverage of McAuliffe headquarters on TV. Everyone seemed shell-shocked. I understood. I'd been there. I guess they saw the writing on the wall before we did.

My race was called at 8:43 p.m., November 2, 2021. I didn't come out and give my acceptance speech until maybe one o'clock the morning of November 3. Why did we wait? We were a team, of course.

Hala Ayala did not call me to concede. At that point, I didn't expect it.

So I called her about eleven o'clock the following day. I was driving through Leesburg on my way home to Winchester. I know what it's like to put your whole heart and soul into an election and not get the result that you wanted. I'd been on the losing end myself. I let her know that she had my ear if she wished to talk at any time. She said to me, "Well, you're my lieutenant governor now. You're the first woman to hold the office. Represent us well."

I told her I would try, and thanked her. So we left it on that good note.

* * *

My victory speech is not one of my favorites. I know it inspired many people because they've told me as much, but I felt it was one of the worst speeches of my life! Maybe I was tired. I gave the speech. I said what was in my heart. I must have looked forlorn as Youngkin gave his acceptance speech because a man at the rope line said to me, "Smile, Winsome, you've just won an election."

There's a lot to campaigning. You have to get your mind in order. You have to encourage your staff and volunteers, find donors, speak to the people. The polls have you down ten points. You have no money. You have to believe yes, it's doable, there is hope!

And you get up the next day and do it all over again.

Campaigns are not sexy. They are intricate, intense, and just hard. They take a toll on your family and business. All of those emotions come into play on election night.

I won by more than fifty thousand votes. Yet, I couldn't wrap my mind around it.

That was when I felt the presence of the Lord. Someone told me, "God is good. You won the election!"

But I knew that if I'd lost He would be the same. He is good. He simply is. I am His child. God is good whether you win or lose.

I gave the speech in a crowded hotel ballroom. There were cameras in this vast block in one section of the room. We had national attention. We were practically the only game in town. Virginia and New Jersey were the only states to have major elections in odd years.

Those news cameras looked like a bunch of one-eyed alien beasts, all turning at the same time.

The crowd was crazy excited. These were our volunteers. They were the ones who had been knocking on the doors. They were the ones who had been praying fervently. They were the ones who had put so much of their lives into this, so much of their time. Our victory was *their* victory. This was *their* night in so many ways. You can lose a campaign all by yourself. All you have to do is open mouth and insert foot. But you can't *win* an election by yourself. These people, these wonderful people, *were* the campaign. You recognize that.

But we didn't just want to speak to them. This was a win for Virginia. We were not just representing Republicans. We were representing Democrats and everybody in between. One Virginia.

I didn't have a speech ready. None at all. I spoke what was in my heart. I told my story. It started with my dad, the man who came to America with $1.75 and a dream. The story of that little girl getting off the plane from Jamaica.

Now here I was. God knows how to do the impossible. He specializes in the impossible. And with His help, I've been doing the impossible all my life.

I was emotional, but I wasn't giddy. I was a long way from giddy.

I felt joy, yes indeed. I ended my speech with that cry of joy, "How sweet it is!"

But I also felt resolute.

I had a job to do.

* * *

Campaigning is one thing. Now it's time to govern. That was Governor-elect Glenn Youngkin's first message after he won. It was time now to govern for all of Virginia.

What I most remember of his speech is how Glenn's son Grant, whom we'd gotten to know well, was jumping for joy, he was so excited and relieved. Campaigning had felt like hell.

Then we all left the stage. I don't know where he and his crew went, but I, my husband, and family went back to our suite and we hit the sack.

I shut my eyes for a brief time, and three hours later I was up and ready for an interview. Then another interview and then another. I think I brushed my teeth. I hope I did.

I'd certainly struck a national nerve on the political left. Left-wing television was abuzz with hatred toward me. It just oozed out. *Saturday Night Live* even mocked me with a ludicrous hit job that more than proved unless you vote Democrat, "you're not Black enough."[1] They also hilariously misjudged the Second Amendment community's support for Black gun ownership.

On the positive side, there was a lot of talk about making history. First female lieutenant governor of Virginia. First immigrant. First female veteran. First time a Black lieutenant governor would be succeeded by a Black lieutenant governor. All in the former capital of the Confederacy, by the way.

I felt this was rather empty gesturing. I wasn't running to make history. That wasn't the point. The identity politics was my opponent's schtick, as a matter of fact. She had continually said she was out to "make history." I don't think people care about that very much. They just want to know who's going to do right by them, the voters.

God doesn't care about history. God has *already* created history. The minute you start making an election about you, you're going to run into problems. It must be about service. I know this sounds clichéd because every politician says it. Okay, some politicians, the only service that you get from them is lip. But watch what we do. It's by that you will know if service is truly in our hearts.

*   *   *

It's very interesting how quickly things change.

When I went to bed we candidates were simply on our own. As soon as he won, the governor-elect was surrounded by security. He and his wife had been whisked from Northern Virginia to Richmond. The next morning I saw on television that they were there, being invited to the governor's mansion by then Governor Northam.

For me, it was media hit after media hit. It was TV after radio after TV after print.

The family and I finally drove back to Winchester.

I learned that Republicans had won the House of Delegates back, as well. The Senate wasn't up for control, but all one hundred seats of the House had been in play. Republicans wanted to celebrate nationwide. They saw hope in Virginia.

Virginia had seemed totally lost to the Democrats. We'd shown how to win.

There were many reasons. We'd pulled in more of the Black vote than ever. We won back the women's vote, which had been leaning Democrat. We did well with Asians and Latinos.

But the main reason we won was parents.

Two years of school shutdowns and masking, two years of Zoom miseducation that had exposed a radical agenda.

When parents saw it on their kids' computers, they recoiled in horror.

Terry McAuliffe had made a fatal error. As Jesus says in Luke, "for of the abundance of the heart his mouth speaketh."[2] In a moment of anger and frustration McAuliffe said parents shouldn't tell teachers what to teach their children.[3] Those words had been the nail in the coffin. He'd opened his mouth and removed all doubt, as they say— all doubt as to where the Democrats stood. Not with parents.

We'd stood with the parents. We stood for real education. That was the real secret sauce to our victory.

On his first day in office, Governor Glenn Youngkin signed eleven executive orders. These included orders ending the use of critical race theory in schools, investigating officials' alleged wrongdoing in Loudoun County, and allowing parents to decide if their children should wear masks in schools.[4] He also created the Commission to Combat Antisemitism, which later produced a comprehensive report.[5]

* * *

One time during the campaign my prayer team decided that we should have a prayer walk across the whole of Virginia. That meant I would have had to stop campaigning and do this prayer walk.

"I can't do that," I told them. "I have to run for office."

But I did take two days off. In Winchester, where I live, we started at George Washington's Fort Loudoun, where he commanded the Virginia militia during the French and Indian War. In Washington's first foray into political office, he won the seat for Frederick County, my county, in the Virginia House of Burgesses, back in colonial times.

The founders from Virginia were flawed and imperfect men. They were touched by God to found a nation where someone like me, someone like you, can be free. Slavery should never have happened. Never!

We are all flawed and imperfect. We are not without sin, not one of us.

When I was a child growing up in Jamaica, it was my job to dust Martin Luther King Jr.'s photo. Every home in Jamaica at the time had a picture of Dr. King in it.

Martin Luther King Jr. came to Jamaica. He said he felt like a human being there.[6] He felt free.

When I was a delegate, I had the chance to meet Dr. King's wife, Coretta Scott King, and take a picture with her. I couldn't believe I was standing next to this woman. There she was planting a tree in his honor in the capital of the former Confederacy.

On Martin Luther King Jr. Day, January 17, 2022, the Virginia senate opened its daily session. I had been newly sworn in. As lieutenant governor, I serve as president of the senate.

I gaveled them in.

EPILOGUE

I was eating breakfast at a hotel in Richmond. The restaurant there happens to have a beautiful view of the capitol.

The girls were between nine and eleven. There were six of them, one celebrating her birthday.

I felt a sort of a listlessness in the group. It was still early morning.

So I went over to their table.

I said, "Ladies, do you know who I am?"

"No."

"I'm the lieutenant governor of Virginia."

"What's that?"

One of the parents said, "It's like being the vice president."

I pointed to the capital. "See that White House–looking building there? That's our capitol, where we make laws."

Just to bring it home, I added, "You've heard of the governor, yes?"

"Right. I'm the number two. Have you studied about the government in school?"

They nodded. Perhaps they had. But I saw a spark of interest. Even a spark of wonder.

I asked, "Have you ever gotten a tour of your capital? That's your government up there. Would you like to take a tour?"

I also asked the moms gathered there, and they said they'd love to do it.

So I made the call and arranged it.

It wasn't anything magical. I just happened to know the tour office number, since I'd done this before. But perhaps it seemed a little magical to those girls. I gave the moms my card to keep in touch.

Guess what? I later got a call. The little girls went on the tour and they loved it.

Before I left the restaurant I told the girls to make sure to include a visit to the governor's mansion on their itinerary. After all, they might be living there one day.

I'm a Black woman, second in command in the former capital of the Confederacy. Virginia is the mother of presidents. Virginia is the mother of states. Virginia is the first permanent English settlement. There's just so much history here. You bump into history everywhere.

Today for the very first time in my life, I looked in the mirror and I saw my grandmother's face. People have always said I look like my father.

Today I saw my grandmother's face in the mirror. I called my mother and I said, "Mom, I saw Mommy in the mirror. What does that mean?"

She said, "Oh, she must be happy with you, happy with what you're doing."

In Jamaica you just want to feel the dirt under your feet, the grass between your toes. In Virginia, in my own yard, I work barefoot most of the time. I'm home in Virginia.

I have not had a normal life. Neither have you, perhaps.

But who says any life is normal? Nothing is normal. What was meant to be was a supernatural relationship with God where we can see him, we can speak freely to him, just as Adam and Eve and Abraham did before, and as did Moses and the prophets.

Adam and Eve had a free one-on-one experience in the Garden of Eden. The curse of sin changed that. We now work by the sweat of our brow and it's hard.[1] The ground won't easily provide for us.

That's not normal. That was never supposed to happen.

We were never supposed to not be able to pay our bills. That's not normal.

We were always supposed to have a mom and a dad.

Women were never supposed to bear children in pain.

Some of us have a better experience than others, but that doesn't mean it's normal. It's not.

We were meant to have a supernatural experience, a direct connection with God, always.

For what purpose were you created? What is the purpose of your being? For a time, I thought it was to reach a goal, you know, find a mission in life, only to discover in Isaiah 43:7 what God says.

"I created you to worship Me."

There it is, plain and simple.

It's like a hammer. Why was it created? To pound.

God created us to worship Him, to have this immediate relationship with Him, but we cut ourselves off from Him. Now we try to find things to fill that hole. And it doesn't work. We look for love in all the wrong places, as the country song goes. Until we reestablish that relationship with God, we will always be aimlessly flailing in the wind. The job can't fill it. Getting married can't fill it. Not even having children can fill it. Not even good health and a long life.

Only a supernatural and complete relationship with God can fill it because that's how He created us. Nothing else will do.

Some people look to government as a supernatural savior. Government can do some things, but it can never do that. And they find other gods. They're seeking something spiritual, and they don't know what they're seeking. You hear about some of these celebrities and all the money in the world and all the cars, all the big houses, all the women, and it doesn't *do it* until they find the Lord. Only God can fill that God-shaped hole in the heart.

As author John L. Mason once said, "You're born an original. Don't die a copy." God has certain plans for your life. These are not everybody else's plans; they're your plans.

You're not defective. You have purpose. You have value.

You're His masterpiece.

NOTES

Chapter Four: Jamaica, Faith, and Jesus

1. The Green Vanguard. "Socialist Michael Manley Wrecked Jamaica!" Facebook, July 18, 2020. https://www.facebook.com/JLPGreenVanguard/videos/socialist-michael -manley-wrecked-jamaica/603936403863246/.

2. Treaster, Joseph B. "Jamaican Vote Sweeps Manley to Power." *New York Times*, February 10, 1989. https://www.nytimes.com/1989/02/10/world/jamaican-vote-sweeps -manley-to-power.html.

3. Priest, Dana. "Bush Hails Jamaica's Manley, Once a Third-World Spokesman." *Washington Post*, May 4, 1990. https://www.washingtonpost.com/archive/politics/1990/05 /04/bush-hails-jamaicas-manley-once-a-third-world-spokesman/f2f72825-b140 -4766-b0bf-9ac370c2851f/.

4. Revelation 3:8 (NIV).

5. I wrote a book on this subject called *Stop Being a Christian Wimp!*, in fact. That book is currently out of print. I want to revise it and add a workbook before reissuing it. But it's coming…one of these days!

Chapter Five: American Teen

1. FoundationINTERVIEWS. "Nichelle Nichols on Martin Luther King, Jr. Convincing Her Not to Leave '*Star Trek*.'" YouTube, video, January 16, 2019. https://www .youtube.com/watch?v=zrzygziT11I.

2. "Nichelle Nichols Remembers Dr. King." *Star Trek* (website), March 7, 2019. https:// intl.startrek.com/news/nichelle-nichols-remembers-dr-king.

3. Wright, Tracy. "'*Star Trek*' Legend Nichelle Nichols' Ashes to Be Launched into Deep Space on Vulcan Rocket." Fox News, August 25, 2022. https://www.foxnews.com /entertainment/star-trek-legend-nichelle-nichols-ashes-launched-into-deep-space-on -vulcan-rocket.

Chapter Six: Boot Camp

1. "Family *Ceratopogonidae*—Biting Midges." BugGuide. Iowa State University. https:// bugguide.net/node/view/19768.

Chapter Seven: The Few. The Proud.

1. "Naturalization Oath of Allegiance to the United States of America." U.S. Citizenship and Immigration Services, updated July 5, 2020. https://www.uscis.gov /citizenship/learn-about-citizenship/the-naturalization-interview-and-test/naturalization -oath-of-allegiance-to-the-united-states-of-america.

Chapter Eight: The Republican Road

1. "Diana Ross: Biography." IMDb. https://www.imdb.com/name/nm0005384/bio.

Chapter Nine: Speaking God's Blessings

1. Wilkinson, Bruce H. *Family Walk: 52 Weekly Devotions for Your Family.* Grand Rapids, MI: Zondervan, 1991. https://faithgateway.com/products/family-walk-52-weekly -devotions-for-your-family.
2. Sears, Winsome Earle. *Stop Being a Christian Wimp!* Maitland, FL: Xulon Press, 2009.
3. Romans 12:6–8 (ESV).
4. Job 38:4–7 (NIV).
5. Deuteronomy 4:23–24, (KJV).
6. Hebrews 12:27–29 (NIV).
7. Matthew 16:24 (NIV).

Chapter Ten: The Storm and the Shelter

1. Here's an example of some of the activities involved: Smith, Susan. "Pair Bring Hope to Victims Shelter Offers Women Support and Training." *Virginian-Pilot* (Norfolk, VA), July 28, 2000, A3. The *Virginian-Pilot* Archives. https://pilotonline.newsbank.com /doc/news/0EAFF23F52436A5E. (A user account is required to access this website.)

Chapter Eleven: The First Campaign

1. Here is some reporting on me when I finally received my degree: Walzer, Philip. "Regent Alumni Make Mark in Latest Election—Victories By-products of Christian School Boost Its Profile in Politics." *Virginian-Pilot* (Norfolk, VA), November 23, 2001, B1. The *Virginian-Pilot* Archives. https://pilotonline.newsbank.com/doc/news /0F00D1A15BE5BC1A.
2. "Vision & Mission." Regent University. https://www.regent.edu/about-regent/vision -mission/.
3. "Welcome to Thelma Drake.com." Thelma Drake (personal website), updated January 2021. http://thelmadrake.com/index.html.
4. Here are a couple of examples:
   - Sears, Winsome. "Letters to Editor—The Virginian-Pilot." *Virginian-Pilot* (Norfolk, VA), September 7, 1998, B10. The *Virginian-Pilot* Archives. https://pilotonline .newsbank.com/doc/news/0EAFFBCE908E5A10.

- Sears, Winsome Earle. "Please Stop Picking on Bush." *Virginian-Pilot* (Norfolk, VA), May 9, 2001, B10. The *Virginian-Pilot* Archives. https://pilotonline.newsbank.com/doc/news/0EBEBC24B82BDA29.

5. "About the Leadership Institute." Leadership Institute. https://www.leadershipinstitute.org/aboutus/.

6. Morton Blackwell (@MortonBlackwell). Twitter. https://twitter.com/MortonBlackwell.

7. The reason why was that incumbent Billy Robinson had faced a serious challenge in the Democratic primary. He was beset with ethics problems right and left. The Republicans sensed a chance against him. Glass, Jon. "Democrats Rally Around Robinson—Edmonds Trial Viewed as Wild Card, Could Hurt or Help the Incumbent." *Virginian-Pilot* (Norfolk, VA), June 1, 1999, B1. The *Virginian-Pilot* Archives. https://pilotonline.newsbank.com/doc/news/0EAFFC7C1B1AC85A.

8. Davis, Marc. "Robinson: Confident Delegate Struts His Campaign Prowess Through Poplar Halls." *Virginian-Pilot* (Norfolk, VA), May 23, 1999, B1. The *Virginian-Pilot* Archives. https://pilotonline.newsbank.com/doc/news/0EAFFC76CE3C57DC.

9. Davis, Marc. "The End of an Era for Norfolk Delegate Robinson Leaves Richmond, Not Politics." *Virginian-Pilot* (Norfolk, VA), December 23, 2001, B5. The *Virginian-Pilot* Archives. https://pilotonline.newsbank.com/doc/news/0F0A0C6A03B29F92.

10. Virginian-Pilot, The. "Former Rep. Billy Robinson Dies at Age 64." *Virginian-Pilot* (Norfolk, VA), December 18, 2006. https://www.pilotonline.com/news/obituaries/article_24176d00-88ce-5fd6-a307-b028f77d4b0e.html.

11. Peter, Jennifer. "In Most Local House Races, Donor Dollars Are Lopsided—Incumbents Win Fund War in Area's Contests." *Virginian-Pilot* (Norfolk, VA), October 27, 2001, A1. The *Virginian-Pilot* Archives. https://pilotonline.newsbank.com/doc/news/0EF6EE40300A1E7C.

12. Davis, Marc, and Cindy Clayton. "House Candidate Accuses Man of Stalking—Sears Says Leader of New Black Panther Party Followed Her He Denies Accusation." *Virginian-Pilot* (Norfolk, VA), November 3, 2001, B3. The *Virginian-Pilot* Archives. https://pilotonline.newsbank.com/doc/news/0EF8E8BD2BE0F60D.

13. Minium, Harry. "Local." *Virginian-Pilot* (Norfolk, VA), May 1, 2010, B1. The *Virginian-Pilot* Archives. https://pilotonline.newsbank.com/doc/news/12F74920C76A7FA0.

14. Davis, Marc. "Candidate Rejects Local Activist's Views—Robinson's Remarks About the Leader of Panther Party Not Enough, Opponent Says." *Virginian-Pilot* (Norfolk, VA), November 3, 2001, B5. The *Virginian-Pilot* Archives. https://pilotonline.newsbank.com/doc/news/0EF9912FF4D8CE25.

15. Clayton, Cindy. "Black Panther Leader Convicted in Case Pursued by Del. Sears." *Virginian-Pilot* (Norfolk, VA), April 17, 2002, B7. The *Virginian-Pilot* Archives. https://pilotonline.newsbank.com/doc/news/0F2F9E08E129BC57.

16. Davis, Marc. "Veteran Sees Challenge from Newcomer in 90th." *Virginian-Pilot* (Norfolk, VA), October 29, 2001, B1. The *Virginian-Pilot* Archives. https://pilotonline.newsbank.com/doc/news/0EF79724FB1928B7.

17. McGlone, Tim. "Del. Sears Says Robinson Got Her Credit Report." *Virginian-Pilot* (Norfolk, VA), July 9, 2003, B2. The *Virginian-Pilot* Archives. https://pilotonline.newsbank.com/doc/news/0FC3426A8B4E58A6.

18. Staff. *Virginian-Pilot* (Norfolk, VA), February 7, 2003, B4. The *Virginian-Pilot* Archives. https://pilotonline.newsbank.com/doc/news/0F912D340535E53E.

19. Hardy, Katrice. *Virginian-Pilot* (Norfolk, VA), January 8, 2004, B2. The *Virginian-Pilot* Archives. https://pilotonline.newsbank.com/doc/news/0FFF96AF1754C9C7.

20. Davis, Marc. "Chesapeake Precincts Decided Sears' Victory." *Virginian-Pilot* (Norfolk, VA), November 8, 2001, A12. The *Virginian-Pilot* Archives. https://pilotonline.newsbank.com/doc/news/0EFAE2DB0C2C89E9.

21. "Virginia Elections Database: Search Elections." Virginia Department of Elections. https://historical.elections.virginia.gov/elections/search/year_from:1947/year_to:2016/office_id:8/district_id:27392.

22. Davis, Marc, and Clint Riley. "Challenger Wins Robinson's Long-Held Seat." *Virginian-Pilot* (Norfolk, VA), November 7, 2001, A1. The *Virginian-Pilot* Archives. https://pilotonline.newsbank.com/doc/news/0EFAE2DADF8DBB82.

23. Davis, Marc. "GOP Helps Bankroll Bid Against Robinson—His Legal Troubles May Benefit Sears." *Virginian-Pilot* (Norfolk, VA), November 1, 2001, B1. The *Virginian-Pilot* Archives. https://pilotonline.newsbank.com/doc/news/0EF8E8BC547F9C8A.

24. Staff Report. "Del. Robinson Misses More Court Dates." *Virginian-Pilot* (Norfolk, VA), October 18, 2001, B10. The *Virginian-Pilot* Archives. https://pilotonline.newsbank.com/doc/news/0EF50F4A397D61F1.

25. Davis, Marc. "Robinson Found in Contempt One Day After Losing District Seat." *Virginian-Pilot* (Norfolk, VA), November 8, 2001, A1. The *Virginian-Pilot* Archives. https://pilotonline.newsbank.com/doc/news/0EFAE2DB0D857FC2.

26. Morse, Gordon C. "Opinion: Sears Nomination Recalls Grim Days for Democrats." *Virginian-Pilot* (Norfolk, VA), May 15, 2021. https://www.pilotonline.com/opinion/columns/vp-ed-column-morse-0516-20210515-q2eoy4qx4zc7fck3p6fnpqsila-story.html.

27. Davis. "Veteran Sees Challenge from Newcomer in 90th."

28. Davis, Marc. "Court Behavior Part of Campaign Robinson's Opponent Slams His Lawyering—He Says It's No Issue." *Virginian-Pilot* (Norfolk, VA), October 16, 2001, B1. The *Virginian-Pilot* Archives. https://pilotonline.newsbank.com/doc/news/0EF34AA7188B0109.

29. Virginian-Pilot, The. "What Happened to Billy Robinson?" *Virginian-Pilot* (Norfolk, VA), June 23, 2006. https://www.pilotonline.com/news/article_199736df-6715-58d0-829a-1d40e3d56b61.html.

30. Nuckols, Christina. "Ms. Sears Goes to Richmond—Norfolk Woman Juggles Roles of Wife, Mother and Now Freshman Legislator." *Virginian-Pilot* (Norfolk, VA), February 6, 2003, B4. The *Virginian-Pilot* Archives. https://pilotonline.newsbank.com /doc/news/0F912D332ABE04DA.

Chapter Twelve: Delegate Sears—I Am Black Enough

1. "A History of the Virginia House of Delegates." House History. Virginia House of Delegates Clerk's Office. https://history.house.virginia.gov/.
2. "Winsome Earle Sears." House History. Virginia House of Delegates Clerk's Office. https://history.house.virginia.gov/members/9873.
3. Washington Times, The. "Sears Quits Black Caucus." *Washington Times*, February 5, 2003. https://www.washingtontimes.com/news/2003/feb/5/20030205-085418 -9498r/.
4. Nuckols. "Ms. Sears Goes to Richmond—Norfolk Woman Juggles Roles of Wife, Mother and Now Freshman Legislator."
5. We see this in the Bible in Job 23:10, as well as in 1 Peter 1:7 and 1 Peter 4:12.
6. "Statement from House Speaker William J. Howell." Virginia House GOP, August 26, 2017. https://virginiahouse.gop/2017/08/26/statement-from-house-speaker-william -j-howell/.
7. "*Black v. Commonwealth*." 262 Va. 764 (Va. 2001), 553 S.E.2d 738. Casetext. https:// casetext.com/case/black-v-commonwealth-3.
8. Incidentally, Jerry Kilgore had a twin in the state legislature at the time. The two men were practically identical, very hard to tell apart when one met them in the hallways.
9. Bob McDonnell later went on to become attorney general and then governor, where he appointed me to the Virginia Board of Education.
10. "Title 18.2. Crimes and Offenses Generally." § 18.2-423.01. Burning Object on Property of Another or a Highway or Other Public Place with Intent to Intimidate; Penalty." LIS Virginia Law. Virginia's Legislative Information System. https://law.lis .virginia.gov/vacode/title18.2/chapter9/section18.2-423.01/.
11. "*Virginia v. Black*." 538 US 343 (2003). Oyez. Accessed January 19, 2023. https:// www.oyez.org/cases/2002/01-1107.
12. "*Virginia v. Black*—Oral Argument—December 11, 2002." Lawaspect.com. https:// lawaspect.com/case-virginia-v-black-transcription-oral-argument-december-11-2002/.
13. A recording of the full hearing can be found here: "Historic Supreme Court Oral Arguments: *Virginia v. Black*." C-SPAN, April 7, 2003. https://www.c-span.org /video/?92790-1%2Fhistoric-supreme-court-oral-arguments-virginia-v-black.
14. Nuckols. "Ms. Sears Goes to Richmond—Norfolk Woman Juggles Roles of Wife, Mother and Now Freshman Legislator."
15. "Charter Schools in Virginia." Ballotpedia, n.d. https://ballotpedia.org/Charter _schools_in_Virginia.

16. "Quick Facts on Charter Schools." Public Schools First NC. https://www.publicschools firstnc.org/resources/fact-sheets/quick-facts-on-charter-schools/.

17. "District of Columbia Charter Schools." National Charter School Resource Center, n.d. https://charterschoolcenter.ed.gov/category/states/district-columbia.

18. Szabo, Liz. "Beach Surgeon Faces State Inquiry Committee Advises Board of Medicine to Consider Allegations." *Virginian-Pilot* (Norfolk, VA), July 27, 2001, A1. The *Virginian-Pilot* Archives. https://pilotonline.newsbank.com/doc/news/0ED897E438148404.

19. Szabo, Liz. "Letter Warned Hospital of Surgeon's Problems." *Virginian-Pilot* (Norfolk, VA), June 27, 2002, A1. The *Virginian-Pilot* Archives. https://pilotonline.newsbank .com/doc/news/0F4704E2F22FF2F5.

20. Virginia General Assembly. Joint Legislative Audit and Review Commission. "Final Report: Review of the Health Regulatory Boards." House Document No. 5. N.d. http://jlarc.virginia.gov/pdfs/reports/Rpt233.pdf.

21. McCabe, Robert. "House OKs Measure to Reform State's Medical Board—Bill Would Give Panel More Disciplinary Tools." *Virginian-Pilot* (Norfolk, VA), January 25, 2003, A1. The *Virginian-Pilot* Archives. https://pilotonline.newsbank.com/doc /news/0F8CE453E457A4D1.

Chapter Thirteen: My Only Opponent Is Me

1. "House Votes on 1999-261." On the Issues, n.d. https://www.ontheissues.org/HouseVote /Party_1999-261.htm.

2. "H.R.4623—Child Obscenity and Pornography Prevention Act of 2002." Congress. gov, n.d. https://www.congress.gov/bill/107th-congress/house-bill/4623/related-bills.

3. "Letter to Reps. Smith and Scott on H.R. 4623, the 'Child Obscenity and Pornography Prevention Act of 2002.'" American Civil Liberties Union, n.d. https://www .aclu.org/letter/letter-reps-smith-and-scott-hr-4623-child-obscenity-and-pornography -prevention-act-2002.

4. "H.R. 4623 (107th): Child Obscenity and Pornography Prevention Act of 2002." GovTrack, June 25, 2002. https://www.govtrack.us/congress/votes/107-2002/h256.

5. "Bobby Scott on Abortion." Updated October 1, 2022. On the Issues https://www .ontheissues.org/VA/Bobby_Scott_Abortion.htm.

6. "Virginia: 2020 Census." United States Census Bureau, June 29, 2022. https://www .census.gov/library/stories/state-by-state/virginia-population-change-between-census -decade.html.

7. Longbons, Tessa. "Abortion Reporting: Virginia (2018)." Charlotte Lozier Institute, June 11, 2021. https://lozierinstitute.org/abortion-reporting-virginia-2018/.

Chapter Fourteen: The Lord Giveth, the Lord Taketh Away

1. Barner, E. M. "Sears Daughter, Granddaughters in Fatal Crash." Bearing Drift, June 6, 2012. https://bearingdrift.com/2012/06/06/sears-daughter-granddaughters-in -fatal-crash/.

2. 2 Corinthians 4:8–9 (NIV).

3. Psalm 23:5 (NIV).

4. For example, in Genesis 16, 19, 21,24, 31, 38 (NIV).

5. Revelation 21:23–25 (NIV).

6. Revelation 21:21 (NIV).

7. Revelation 4 (NIV).

8. Revelation 5:5–8 (NIV).

9. Isaiah 6:1 (NIV).

10. Isaiah 6:4 (NIV).

11. Ezekiel 10:14 (NIV).

12. Isaiah 6:2 (NIV).

13. Jude 1:9.

14. Job 1 (NIV).

Chapter Sixteen: Sense and Sensibility

1. Nuckols, Christina. "Winsome on Board, a Gadfly by Nature." *Virginian-Pilot* (Norfolk, VA), April 24, 2011, B10. The *Virginian-Pilot* Archives. https://pilotonline .newsbank.com/doc/news/136D9C04F2E0A0B0.

2. Quoted in *More Maxims of Mark*. Ed. Merle Johnson. 1925. The quote is also discussed here: "Clothes Make the Man. Naked People Have Little or No Influence in Society." Quote Investigator, November 13, 2018. https://quoteinvestigator .com/2012/05/04/twain-clothes/.

3. Blanks, Walter Jr. "Teachers' Unions Deserve Much of the Blame for Pandemic-Era Learning Loss." *National Review*, September 6, 2022. https://www.nationalreview.com /2022/09/teachers-unions-deserve-much-of-the-blame-for-pandemic-era-learning-loss/.

4. There are many reports on detrimental effects of making kids wear masks including:

   • Green, Erica L. "The Students Returned, but the Fallout from a Long Disruption Remained." *New York Times*, December 24, 2021. https://www.nytimes .com/2021/12/24/us/politics/covid-school-reopening-teen-mental-health.html.

   • Makary, Marty, and H. Cody Meissner. "Opinion: The Case Against Masks for Children." *Wall Street Journal*, August 8, 2021. https://www.wsj.com/articles /masks-children-parenting-schools-mandates-covid-19-coronavirus-pandemic -biden-administration-cdc-11628432716.

   • Oster, Emily. "Kids and Masks." ParentData, November 8, 2021. https://www .parentdata.org/p/kids-and-masks.

   • Leonhardt, David. "Maskless and Inaccurate." *New York Times*, January 14, 2022. https://www.nytimes.com/2022/01/14/briefing/supreme-court-covid-mask -mandate.html.

   • Martin, Naomi. "What Happens When Students Remove Masks? These Mass. Schools Are Finding Out." *Boston Globe*, January 4, 2022. https://www

.bostonglobe.com/2021/12/19/metro/what-happens-when-students-remove-masks
-these-mass-schools-are-finding-out/.

- Prasad, Vinay. "The Cult of Masked Schoolchildren." *Tablet Magazine*, January 20, 2022. https://www.tabletmag.com/sections/science/articles/cult-masked
-schoolchildren.
- Fagan, Laura. "Have San Francisco Policies Done More Harm to Children than COVID?" *SFGate*, January 20, 2022. https://www.sfgate.com/politics-op-eds
/article/San-Francisco-policies-COVID-children-mask-school-16787963.php.

Here is a comprehensive overview from Justin Hart's extraordinary and ground-breaking Rational Ground group:

Burns, Emily. "Un-Masking Children: Part 1 of 4. The Role of Children in COVID-19 Transmission in Schools." Rational Ground, May 11, 2021. https://rationalground
.com/un-masking-children-part-1-of-4-the-role-of-children-in-covid-19-transmission
-in-schools/.

Chapter Seventeen: Representing the Cause

1. Sweet, Lynn. "How Holocaust Denier Jones Got on Ballot: Illinois GOP Let Guard Down." *Chicago Sun-Times*, April 7, 2018. https://web.archive.org/web/20180612143714
/https://chicago.suntimes.com/news/how-holocaust-denier-jones-got-on-ballot-illinois
-gop-let-guard-down/.

2. Olivo, Antonio. "Provocative Things That U.S. Senate GOP Candidate Corey Stewart Has Said." *Washington Post*, July 1, 2018. https://www.washingtonpost.com/graphics
/2018/local/amp-stories/provocative-things-that-corey-stewart-has-said-and-done/.

3. Jacobs, Ben, and Martin Pengelly. "Steve Bannon Cuts Ties with Far-Right Candidate Trying to Unseat Paul Ryan." *Guardian*, December 27, 2017. https://www
.theguardian.com/world/2017/dec/27/steve-bannon-paul-nehlen-paul-ryan.

4. Crowe, Jack. "Ralph Northam Med-School-Yearbook Page Shows Blackface, KKK Photo." *National Review Online*, February 1, 2019. Yahoo! News. https://news.yahoo
.com/ralph-northam-med-school-yearbook-212644346.html.

5. Steinbuch, Yaron. "Virginia Lt. Gov. Justin Fairfax's Sex Assault Accusers Speak Out: 'It Was a Huge Betrayal.'" *New York Post*, April 2, 2019. https://nypost.com/2019/04/02
/virginia-lt-gov-justin-fairfaxs-sex-assault-accusers-speak-out-it-was-a-huge-betrayal/.

6. Singman, Brooke. "Virginia Lt. Gov. Justin Fairfax's Accuser Releases Statement Detailing Sexual-Assault Allegations." Fox News, February 6, 2019. https://www
.foxnews.com/politics/virginia-lt-gov-justin-fairfax-sexual-assault-accuser-releases
-statement-detailing-allegations.

7. "Accuser Says Justin Fairfax Referenced Her Prior Alleged Sexual Assault, Said She'd Be 'Too Afraid' to Report It." CBS News, April 2, 2019. https://www.cbsnews.com
/news/justin-fairfax-accuser-meredith-watson-says-he-targeted-her-because-she-was
-allegedly-assaulted-before/.

8. Pappas, Alex. "Virginia AG Mark Herring Admits Wearing Blackface at 1980 College Party." Fox News, February 6, 2019. https://www.foxnews.com/politics/virginia -ag-mark-herring-admits-wearing-blackface-at-1980-college-party.

9. Michel, Adam. "An Economic History of the Tax Cuts and Jobs Act: Higher Wages, More Jobs, New Investment." The Heritage Foundation, March 16, 2021. https:// www.heritage.org/taxes/report/economic-history-the-tax-cuts-and-jobs-act-higher -wages-more-jobs-new-investment.

10. Wall Street Journal, The. "Clinton's Email Deceptions." *Wall Street Journal*, May 25, 2016. https://www.wsj.com/articles/clintons-email-deceptions-1464219303.

11. "Statement by FBI Director James B. Comey on the Investigation of Secretary Hillary Clinton's Use of a Personal E-Mail System." FBI, July 5, 2016. https://www.fbi.gov /news/press-releases/press-releases/statement-by-fbi-director-james-b-comey-on-the -investigation-of-secretary-hillary-clinton2019s-use-of-a-personal-e-mail-system.

12. Smith, Samuel. "Trump Signs Prison Reform Bill First Step Act: 'Everybody Said It Couldn't Be Done.'" *Christian Post*, December 21, 2018. https://www .christianpost.com/news/trump-signs-prison-reform-bill-first-step-act-everybody -said-it-couldnt-be-done.html.

13. Thomsen, Jacqueline. "Education Dept Forgives Relief Loans Given to Black Colleges After Hurricanes." *Hill*, March 14, 2018. https://thehill.com/homenews /administration/378472-education-dept-fully-forgives-relief-loans-given-to-hbcus-after/.

14. Olson, Bradley. "U.S. Becomes Net Exporter of Oil, Fuels for First Time in Decades." *Wall Street Journal*, December 6, 2018. https://www.wsj.com/articles/u-s-becomes -net-exporter-of-oil-fuels-for-first-time-in-decades-1544128404.

15. Quinn, Jimmy. "Pompeo Predicts 'Many' More Mideast Peace Deals: 'We Broke Glass.'" *National Review*, November 23, 2020. https://www.nationalreview.com/2020 /11/pompeo-predicts-many-more-mideast-peace-deals-we-broke-glass/.

16. CNN. "Donald Trump: 'Look at My African-American over Here...'" YouTube, video, June 3, 2016. https://www.youtube.com/watch?v=rOYMFkFgPzk.

17. Fox News. "Trump Attacks McCain's Record as War Hero, Draws Rebuke from GOP Presidential Field." Fox News, December 20, 2015. https://www.foxnews.com /politics/trump-attacks-mccains-record-as-war-hero-draws-rebuke-from-gop -presidential-field.

18. Numbers 22:31–33 (KJV).

19. 2 Chronicles 12:12 (NIV).

20. WFMYStaff. "Vernon Robinson Among Nation's Most Successful Fundraisers." wfmynews2.com. WFMY News 2, July 17, 2006. https://www.wfmynews2.com/article /news/local/vernon-robinson-among-nations-most-successful-fundraisers/83-403289301.

21. Fox News. "Blumenthal Apologizes for Inaccurate Claims about Vietnam Service." Fox News, December 23, 2015. https://www.foxnews.com/politics/blumenthal-apologizes -for-inaccurate-claims-about-vietnam-service.

22. Washington Times, The. "Editorial: Richard Blumenthal's Rolling Blunder." *Washington Times*, May 21, 2010. https://www.washingtontimes.com/news/2010/may/21/richard-blumenthals-rolling-blunder/.

23. These include allegations of influence peddling in both Russia and China. A couple of infamous examples can be found here: Morris, Emma-Jo, and Gabrielle Fonrouge. "Emails Reveal How Hunter Biden Tried to Cash in Big on Behalf of Family with Chinese Firm." *New York Post*, October 15, 2020. https://nypost.com/2020/10/15/emails-reveal-how-hunter-biden-tried-to-cash-in-big-with-chinese-firm/. And here: Devine, Miranda, and Emily Crane. "Hunter Biden–Linked Real Estate Firm Got at Least $100M from Russian Oligarch: Sources." *New York Post*, October 17, 2022. https://nypost.com/2022/10/17/hunter-bidens-real-estate-firm-received-over-100m-from-russian-oligarch/.

24. Orwell, George. *Animal Farm: A Fairy Story* 1945; HMH Books. Kindle Edition.

25. Joshua 5:13 (NIV).

26. Joshua 5:14 (NIV).

27. Joshua 5:15 (NIV).

28. Here's a prime example: Vincent, Isabel, and Joshua Rhett Miller. "Inside the $6M Mansion BLM Reportedly Bought with Donated Funds." *New York Post*, April 5, 2022. https://nypost.com/2022/04/05/the-6-million-mansion-blm-reportedly-bought-with-donated-funds/.

29. When remembering this, I sometimes conflate the GNB and ESV translations. I like the word "opponents" better than "enemies" in this context: Philippians 1:28–30 (GNB).

Chapter Eighteen: The Nomination

1. Bedard, Paul. "Boom: 21M Guns Sold in 2020, up 60%, Women, Blacks Top Buyers." *Washington Examiner*, January 13, 2021. https://www.washingtonexaminer.com/washington-secrets/boom-21-million-guns-sold-in-2020-up-60-women-blacks-top-buyers.

2. Watson, Steve. "Report: The 'Squad' Hired Private Security While Calling for Abolition of Police." *Summit News*, April 22, 2021. https://summit.news/2021/04/22/report-the-squad-hired-private-security-while-calling-for-abolition-of-police/.

3. Hawkins, AWR. "Martin Luther King Applied to Carry Concealed for Self-Defense but Was Denied." Gun Owners of America, January 17, 2017. https://www.gunowners.org/mlk-denied-concealed-carry-permit/.

4. There were 125 voting units in the state. Convention delegates represented a respective voting unit. Each voting unit was allocated a set number of delegate votes calculated as one delegate vote per every 250 votes cast for the Republican candidate in the most recent major election. In the end, the 125 voting units divided 12,554 delegate votes. Voters fill out a single ballot that ranks their preferences. Votes were counted. In each round, the two candidates who received the fewest votes were

eliminated, and their voters were reallocated based on their stated preferences for the other candidates. This went on until a candidate received more than 50 percent of the ballots. The voting unit delegates then cast their selections of the candidates. The result was the candidate who received the most delegate votes statewide won the nomination.

5. "The GOP's Convoluted Nomination Process." The Virginia Public Access Project, March 31, 2021. https://www.vpap.org/visuals/visual/gop-convention-voting-rules/.

6. "Virginia Lieutenant Gubernatorial Election, 2021 (May 8 Republican Convention)." Ballotpedia. https://ballotpedia.org/Virginia_lieutenant_gubernatorial_election ,_2021_(May_8_Republican_convention)#cite_note-gopcall-49.

Chapter Nineteen: How Sweet It Is!

1. Newsmax. "Fake News Media Calls Winsome Sears 'Black Mouth' of White Supremacy; Greg Kelly Reports." YouTube, video, November 5, 2021. https://www .youtube.com/watch?v=TF_3KKwZ6I0.

2. There are many, many examples. Here's one of the more famous ones: Rutz, David, and Brandon Gillespie. "Liberal MSNBC Guest Calls Winsome Sears a 'Black Mouth' for 'White Supremacist Practices.'" Fox News, November 5, 2021. https://www.foxnews .com/media/liberal-dyson-msnbc-joy-reid-winsome-sears-black-mouth-white -supremacist.

3. Steinhauser, Paul. "Biden Says 'You Ain't Black' If Torn Between Him and Trump, in Dustup with Charlamagne tha God." Fox News, May 22, 2020. https://www.foxnews .com/politics/biden-torn-him-and-trump-aint-black-in-dust-up-with-charlamagne -tha-god.

4. Pollak, Joel B. "Joe Biden: 'Unlike the African American Community…the Latino Community Is an Incredibly Diverse Community.'" Breitbart, August 6, 2020. https:// www.breitbart.com/politics/2020/08/06/joe-biden-unlike-the-african-american -community-the-latino-community-is-an-incredibly-diverse-community-nabj/.

5. For example, here's a report on lowering math scores in Virginia: Dorman, Sam. "Virginia DOE Pushes Document on 'Mathematics Through the Lens of Social Justice.'" Fox News, April 23, 2021. https://www.foxnews.com/us/virginia-math-lens-social -justice-race. Here's one on lowering required social studies standards: Seymour, Liz. "Va. Lowers Passing Score for Some SOL Tests." Washington Post, November 28, 2001. https://www.washingtonpost.com/archive/local/2001/11/28/va-lowers-passing -score-for-some-sol-tests/79297f7d-9f95-48c6-8d9c-345db972d234/.

6. See, for example, Chris Rufo's excellent reporting, such as: Rufo, Christopher F. "Critical Race Theory in Education." Christopher Rufo (personal website), April 27, 2021. https://christopherrufo.com/critical-race-theory-in-education/.

7. Clark, Chrissy. "Nation's Largest Teachers Union Says It Will Teach Critical Race Theory in All 50 States, 14,000 School Districts." Daily Wire, July 5, 2021. https://

www.dailywire.com/news/nations-largest-teachers-union-says-it-will-teach-critical-race-theory-in-all-50-states-1400-school-districts.

8. This is sometimes called "Loudon County Bingo": Cho, Aimee. " 'Privilege Bingo' in Fairfax Co. Class Meets Controversy for Including Being a Military Kid." NBC4 Washington, updated January 21, 2022. https://www.nbcwashington.com/news/local/northern-virginia/privilege-bingo-in-fairfax-co-class-meets-controversy-after-it-includes-being-a-military-kid/2942443/.

9. Taft, Victoria. "FBI Used Terrorism Laws to Investigate 'Dozens' of 'Concerned Parents' Who Attended School Board Meetings." PJ Media, May 12, 2022. https://pjmedia.com/news-and-politics/victoria-taft/2022/05/12/fbi-used-terrorism-laws-to-investigate-dozens-of-concerned-parents-who-attended-school-board-meetings-n1597389.

10. "Virginia Mom Says Federal Agents, Helicopter Arrived at School Board Meeting: 'Ridiculously Un-American.' " *Fox and Friends*, Fox News, video, October 27, 2021. https://www.foxnews.com/video/6279038328001.

11. Rosiak, Luke. "Loudoun County Schools Tried To Conceal Sexual Assault Against Daughter in Bathroom, Father Says." *Daily Wire*, October 11, 2021. https://www.dailywire.com/news/loudoun-county-schools-tried-to-conceal-sexual-assault-against-daughter-in-bathroom-father-says.

12. Rosiak. "Loudoun County Schools Tried to Conceal Sexual Assault Against Daughter in Bathroom, Father Says."

13. Taylor, Scott. "Loudoun County Assault Victim's Dad Wants Apology for Being Called 'Domestic Terrorist.' " WJLA. https://wjla.com/features/i-team/loudoun-county-public-school-parents-called-domestic-terrorists-scott-smith-sex-assault-victim-father-wants-apology.

14. Rosiak, Luke. "School District Reinstates Notorious Raunchy Books, Saying 'Gender Queer' Comic Is 'Scientifically Based.' " *Daily Wire*, November 23, 2021. https://www.dailywire.com/news/school-district-reinstates-notorious-raunchy-books-saying-gender-queer-comic-is-scientifically-based.

15. Rosiak, Luke. "American Library Association Pushing Shockingly Obscene Comics on Schoolkids." *Daily Wire*, September 22, 2021. https://www.dailywire.com/news/american-library-association-transgender-gender-queer-comics-schools.

16. Kyrylenko, Veronika. "Pornography in the Classroom? Sexually Explicit Material in Virginia Schools Sparks Outrage Among Parents." *New American*, May 15, 2021. https://thenewamerican.com/pornography-in-the-classroom-sexually-explicit-material-in-virginia-schools-sparks-outrage-among-parents/.

17. Dumas, Breck. "Virginia Mom Confronts School Board over Graphic Sexual Materials in School." Fox News, September 24, 2021. https://www.foxnews.com/us/fairfax-mom-confronts-school-board-over-graphic-sexual-materials-in-school.

18. Rosiak. "School District Reinstates Notorious Raunchy Books, Saying 'Gender Queer' Comic Is 'Scientifically Based.'"

19. Rosiak, Luke. "Watch: School Board Squirms as Mom Reads Them the Gay Porn in Books Available to Students." *Daily Wire*, September 23, 2021. https://www.dailywire .com/news/watch-mom-reads-graphic-gay-porn-found-in-school-library-to-school-board.

20. "Fourth-Graders Who Scored Below Proficient Reading Level by Race and Ethnicity in the United States." Kids Count Data Center. The Annie E. Casey Foundation. https://datacenter.kidscount.org/data/tables/5126-fourth-graders-who-scored-below -proficient-reading-level-by-race-and-ethnicity#detailed/1/any/false/1095,1729,871 ,573,36,867,38,18,16/10,168,9,12,185,107/11557.

21. National Assessment of Educational Progress. "The Nation's Report Card: NAEP." National Center for Education Statistics. https://nces.ed.gov/nationsreportcard/.

22. "Show Me." Search results for 2021 Virginia gubernatorial election. FollowTheMoney .org. https://www.followthemoney.org/show-me?s=VA&y=2021&c-r-ot=G& amp;gro=c-t-id.

23. Opportunity Matters Fund. "Senator Tim Scott: A Vote for Youngkin and Sears Is a Vote for Parents and Their Kids." YouTube, video, October 29, 2021. https://www .youtube.com/watch?v=1GCFPbDvKDE.

24. Olivo, Antonio. "Back in the Virginia Political Spotlight, Winsome Sears Seeks to Lift GOP in Bid for Lieutenant Governor." *Washington Post*, October 16, 2021. https:// www.washingtonpost.com/local/virginia-politics/winsome-sears-virginia-lieutenant -governor/2021/10/15/002d1004-26b9-11ec-8831-a31e7b3de188_story.html.

25. My green juice consists of at least seven different vegetables. This is hardcore. I put in a huge head of fennel. I put in mustard greens, raw and uncooked. I add a bunch of cilantro and a big bunch of dill. I have a huge bunch of bok choy. Also garlic, one clove. I blend all this and make enough for a week or so. It's thick and vegetably. I should get a medal every day I drink this. I normally get twelve ounces out of it. I rotate. I drink one group of vegetables for a while, then rotate to a different set. Whatever makes it bitter—you need that. I'm telling you, within five minutes of drinking it, my eyes open up and I have a massive amount of energy. My slogan? I drink more vegetables in one day than most eat in a whole week.

Chapter Twenty: A Job to Do

1. Colion Noir. "*SNL* Mocks Lt Governor Winsome Sears Because She's Black, Republican, & Pro 2A." YouTube, video, November 9, 2021. https://www.youtube.com /watch?v=YzY5IPi3l4g&t=5s.

2. Luke 6:45 (KJV).

3. Fleetwood, Shawn. "Terry McAuliffe Says Parents Shouldn't Be Telling Schools What to Teach Their Kids." *Federalist*, September 29, 2021. https://thefederalist

.com/2021/09/29/terry-mcauliffe-says-parents-shouldnt-be-telling-schools-what
-to-teach-their-kids/.

4. Brown, Jon. "Virginia Lt. Gov. Winsome Sears Uses Leather High Heel to Gavel in Senate After Gavel Goes Missing." Fox News, February 15, 2022. https://www.foxnews.com/politics/virginia-lt-gov-winsome-sears-leather-high-heel-gavel-senate.

5. Fox 5 DC Digital Team. "Nearly 350 Antisemitic Acts in Virginia so Far in 2022." Fox 5 DC, December 5, 2022. https://www.fox5dc.com/news/nearly-350-antisemitic-acts-in-virginia-so-far-in-2022.

6. Korney, Stephanie. "10 Things to Know About the Visit of Dr Martin Luther King Jr. to Jamaica." Jamaicans.com, January 18, 2021. https://jamaicans.com/10-things-to-know-about-the-visit-of-martin-luther-king-jr-to-jamaica/.

Epilogue

1. Genesis 3:19 (NIV).

ABOUT THE AUTHOR

Virginia Lieutenant Governor **Winsome Earle-Sears** was born in Kingston, Jamaica, in 1964. She is a mother and wife, and is proud to have served in the United States Marines. She was also a hard-charging vice president of the Virginia State Board of Education, and she received presidential appointments to the U.S. Census Bureau, where she cochaired the African American Committee, and the Advisory Committee on Women Veterans to the Secretary of Veterans Affairs.

In addition to earning a master's degree in organizational leadership from Regent University, Earle-Sears built a successful business as a trained electrician. She understands the importance of helping small businesses thrive but is most proud of her community work leading a men's prison ministry and serving as director of a women's homeless shelter for the Salvation Army.